Shakespeare's

WORLD
of
WAR

THE DIRECTOR'S SHAKESPEARE SERIES
by Richard Courtney

SHAKESPEARE'S WORLD OF WAR
Henry VI, Parts 1, 2 & 3, Richard III, King John, Titus Andronicus

SHAKESPEARE'S COMIC WORLD
The Comedy of Errors, The Taming of the Shrew,
The Two Gentlemen of Verona, Love's Labour's Lost,
A Midsummer Night's Dream, The Merchant of Venice

SHAKESPEARE'S WORLD OF DEATH
Romeo and Juliet, Julius Caesar, Hamlet

SHAKESPEARE'S WORLD OF LOVE
Much Ado About Nothing, As You Like It, Twelfth Night,
The Merry Wives of Windsor

SHAKESPEARE'S MASKED WORLD
Richard II, Henry IV, Parts 1 & 2, Henry V

SHAKESPEARE'S PROBLEM WORLD
All's Well That Ends Well, Measure for Measure,
Troilus and Cressida, Timon of Athens, Coriolanus

SHAKESPEARE'S TRAGIC WORLD
Antony and Cleopatra, Macbeth, Othello, King Lear

SHAKESPEARE'S MAGIC WORLD
Pericles, Cymbeline, The Winter's Tale, The Tempest, Henry VIII,
Two Noble Kinsmen

Shakespeare's

WORLD
of
WAR
THE EARLY HISTORIES

Henry VI, Parts 1, 2 & 3
Richard III
King John
Titus Andronicus

RICHARD COURTNEY
Series Editor: Barry Thorne

 SIMON & PIERRE

General Editor: Marian M. Wilson
Series Editor: Barry Thorne
Copy Editor: Jean Paton
Design: Andy Tong
Printed and Bound in Canada by Metrolitho Inc., Quebec

All quotations from Shakespeare's plays are from the New Penguin edition, except as
noted in *End Notes*. Illustrations on pages 172-174 by Richard Courtney.

The writing of this manuscript and the publication of this book were made possible by
support from several sources. We would like to acknowledge the generous assistance
and ongoing support of the **Canada Council**, the **Book Publishing Industry
Development Program** of the **Department of Canadian Heritage**, the **Ontario Arts
Council**, and the **Ontario Publishing Centre** of the **Ministry of Culture, Tourism and
Recreation**.

J. Kirk Howard, President

ISBN 0-88924-229-1
1 2 3 4 5 • 9 7 8 6 5

Canadian Cataloguing in Publication Data
Courtney, Richard

   Shakespeare's world of war : the early histories

(The Director's Shakespeare series)
Includes bibliographical references.
ISBN 0-88924-229-1

1. Shakespeare, William, 1564-1616 — Histories.
2. Shakespeare, William, 1564-1616 — Dramatic
production. I. Title. II. Series.

PR2982.C68 1994   822.3'3   C94-930559-6

Order from Simon & Pierre Publishing Co. Ltd.

2181 Queen Street East	73 Lime Walk	1823 Maryland Avenue
Suite 301	Headington, Oxford	P.O. Box 1000
Toronto, Canada	England	Niagara Falls, N.Y.
M4E 1E5	0X3 7AD	U.S.A. 14302-1000

We are such stuff
As dreams are made on; and our little life
Is rounded with a sleep.   *(The Tempest,* IV.i.156-158)

for

G. WILSON KNIGHT, C.B.E.
In Memoriam

CONTENTS

London's most exciting new stage is being built on the south bank of the
Thames, where The Shakespeare Globe Trust is recreating Shakespeare's
Globe Theatre. Elizabethan building techniques are being used in this
authentic recreation.

The Shakespeare Globe Trust is dedicated to the study, appreciation and
excellence in performance of Shakespeare's plays and to the faithful reconstruction of his Globe Playhouse near its original London Bankside site, as
part of an international, educational and cultural resource centre for people
everywhere. Further information is available from: The Shakespeare Globe
Trust, Bear Gardens, Bankside, Southwark, London SE1 9EB England.

The photograph shows a model of the theatre and other buildings in the
International Shakespeare Globe Centre.

PREFACE

This series of books is intended as an introduction to the plays of William Shakespeare. It is written for stage directors, theatregoers and readers who need to find their way about the plays.

As an actor and director of many of the plays, I have taken a rather different perspective on them: first, that they can only be adequately understood as scripts intended for performance by players; and second, that they focus on the greatest of all themes, the nature of life and death. The first allows us to grasp how the plays *work*. The second demonstrates one reason why Shakespeare's plays are regarded so highly: they address the key issues of our own and every other era by showing that they are universal to humanity in all ages.

The series has a common Introduction and End Notes, which provide basic information for understanding the plays. Acts, scenes, and lines are indicated by round brackets. These divisions into Acts and scenes were added by neo-classical scholars years after Shakespeare's death. But Shakespeare did not intend his plays to be chopped up into small segments. In his time they were played on an unlocalized stage, with one scene flowing into the next.

To recapture this undulation, the plays are examined in the large rhythmical Movements so necessary if they are to be performed. In the theatre, each scene is divided into *beats,* or small rhythmic units; groups of beats with similar emotional effects are *rhythms* (of one or more scenes or within a scene); and groups of these rhythms are *Movements*. In addition, *timing* ranges between fast and slow, and *pace* is the way in which elements of timing are put together.

It is forty years since I first began to direct and act these plays, and almost as long since I began teaching students about them. As a result, I owe much to far more people than I can thank here. But I am under the greatest obligation to the late Professor G. Wilson Knight, for his encouragement and help with my early Shakespearean productions, for the warmth of his personal friendship over several decades, and for his inspiration as an interpreter of Shakespeare. I am grateful to the late Professor Bonamy Dobrée, for his enthusiastic support of my work in directing classic and modern plays; Derek Boughton, for his invaluable support as assistant director in several productions; Philip Stone, the late John Linstrum, Zelda Black, Jacqueline Heywood, Jean Terry Robertson, James Curran, Dorothy Chillingsworth, and other members of experimental drama groups who have worked with me in performances or prepared rehearsals to discover practical ways to overcome specific "knots" in plays; the many players and technical artists, young and old (but particularly the young who continually demonstrate how fresh these plays are), for the long hours we have worked to interpret Shakespeare's plays in the theatre, or in practical interpretation in the classroom. Mention must be made of members of audiences in Britain, Europe, and North America, not just for the warmth of their reactions but specifically for their helpful comments. My thanks also to Sandra M. Burroughs, who typed up the notes for these books; to my wife, Rosemary Courtney, for her usual exemplary editing skills; and to Dr. Barry Thorne, for his expertise.

R. C.
Toronto and
Jackson's Point

INTRODUCTION

READING SHAKESPEARE

The plays of William Shakespeare are among the greatest human achievements. His comedies are funny, his tragedies make us weep, his adventures thrill, amaze and provide us with meaningful experiences. But Shakespeare also means to entertain us.

This does not always happen. Too often, in schools and universities, the plays can be boring, when teachers stop the action to seek out the meaning of a word or discuss the plays like novels. They are *not* novels. We can even be bored in a performance if the actors do not relish Shakespeare, or if they speak his poetry as if it were the telephone directory. The *very last* thing we should be with Shakespeare is bored!

PRINCIPLES

Shakespeare created his plays for *living performance*. They are not "fixed" like a novel, which is the same each time you read it, even if *you* change. One performance of *Hamlet* is never the same as another. Shakespeare wrote his plays for the players who are to act them, for the stage where the people are to come alive, and for the audience who attends them. When we read his plays, or see them in a playhouse, they should excite us. We should be carried along with the action, eagerly waiting for the next thrilling moment. If we are bored in the theatre, we are at a bad performance. If we are bored when we read them, we are reading them badly.

There are two complementary ways of reading Shakespeare's plays: as practical working scripts and as works of artistic meaning. Both ways are complementary. If we read them *only* as working scripts for actors, we may misjudge their significance. If we think of them *only* as great poetry with imaginative meanings, we may miss how they work in practice. But if we read them as living entities we combine both methods.

Shakespeare was the leading dramatist of a working professional company: the Lord Chamberlain's Men in Queen Elizabeth I's time, called the King's Men in the reign of James I. Shakespeare was a part-owner of the company. He acted in his own plays and those of others; he may have played the Ghost in *Hamlet*, and he might have "doubled" it with the First Gravedigger. Perhaps. We will never know for certain. But we do know that he was a man of the theatre.

When we read Shakespeare, his play is not simply a story, and we cannot read it as one. We must do what Shakespeare did: we must imagine "in our mind's eye" the events happening, alive and active, performed by actors on an actual stage. We should imagine where they stand, or where they move. If one is to sit on a throne, where will it be? Actors on a stage are *the medium* through which Shakespeare's genius works. As readers, we must focus on the actors and use our imagination, as Ben Jonson said in *The New Inne* (1629):

> I imagine all the world's a play;
> The state, and men's affairs, all passages
> Of life, to spring new scenes, come in, go out,
> And shift, and vanish; and if I have got
> A seat, to sit at ease here, i'mine Inn,
> To see the comedy ...
> Why, will you envy me my happiness?   (I.iii.128-137)

This passage, with its echoes of Shakespeare's more famous:

> All the world's a stage,
> And all the men and women merely players ...
> *(As You Like It*, II.vii.140-141)

tells us that the stage is Shakespeare's world. Even King Lear can lament:

> When we are born, we cry that we are come
> To this great stage of fools.   (IV.vi.183-184)

If, as we read, we people the stage with actors in roles, we find out about other human beings: their feelings, their experiences, their manner of living. Then the plays are so engrossing that we can hardly put them down.

But as we study them, more ideas will dawn on us. Perhaps we gain more understanding of the crown, or storms and the sea — always important concepts for Shakespeare. *We must allow our imagination the freedom to understand Shakespeare's artistic* *meanings.* We cannot always put these meanings into words, but as Michael Polanyi says: "We know more than we can tell."* Poetic and symbolic meanings give artistic significance. Putting them into words is the business of criticism. We cannot always use language when we appreciate a play, but we should realize that we are absorbing unconscious meanings.

FINDING PRACTICAL MEANING

When we read a play, we use imagination. Thinking "as if" is imagining. But in order to imagine well, we must understand the basic issues when a dramatist writes for the stage.

RECOGNIZING "THE GAP"

Like other great dramatists who are men of the theatre — and we have such examples as Sophocles, Molière, and Goldoni — Shakespeare wrote plays which have *"a natural gap" between the meaning the words have in themselves and the meaning which the performers give them.* A great playwright knows the skills of actors and the meanings they can convey. In the same way that a composer creates a score, the dramatist writes a play for others to interpret. The words on the page provide one kind of meaning: they are the skeleton for a performance. When the actors speak the text they provide a meaning that gives the skeleton flesh and blood — and life. But the meaning which one actor conveys is not necessarily the same as that of another actor in the same role. They are different people; they have different thoughts, ideas, feelings and emotions. In my production of *The Taming of the Shrew* (Leeds University, 1954), I played Christopher Sly in the Induction; when we took it to Germany the same year, the actor playing Gremio was not available, so I had to double the two parts. This doubling provided a new balance to the ensemble, and people who saw both thought it emphasized different meanings. We must allow for "the gap" as we read Shakespeare's plays, and imagine the play taking place before us.

---

* *Personal Knowledge* (New York: Harper, 1964) 6.

FILLING IN THE MEANING

Then we "fill in" the meanings given to us by the text. We re-create the possibilities of the script within the *play world,* an imagined world in which people (performed by actors) live and breathe. This type of re-creation forms a major contrast with the novel. The printed novel, as we read it, is also a fictional "world," but it is a work of art in itself. The *play world* is not. A great dramatist writes the script so that we can "fill in" the meanings, and only then is it a work of art. We "fill in" the meanings on several levels.

On LEVEL 1 we imagine the events "as if" actors are playing them "here and now," in both space and time. We do so through questions that actors and directors ask. Where does the first scene in *Hamlet* take place? What does it look like? What is the atmosphere? What does each actor do there, moment by moment? Does the atmosphere change during the scene? How do we *feel* "now" in comparison with how we felt a minute ago? *Space and time are the key issues to address in any play.*

These questions lead to LEVEL 2. At this level we reach *questions that are specifically asked by actors,* such as:

- What does Hamlet *think* as he says, "To be or not to be"? "To live" or "not to live" is an important question. Hamlet must be in great personal difficulties to ask himself that. He then asks if it is "nobler" to do one thing rather than another. What does he mean by "nobler"? Actors have to know what people *mean* before they can adequately perform roles.
- Is there a distinction between what the person *thinks* and what he *says?* In some cases there is a difference. When Richard of Gloucester tells his brother Clarence he will help him while he is in the Tower of London, he is lying — he is actually about to arrange for him to be killed.
- Is there a distinction between what the person *consciously thinks* and what he means *unconsciously?* When Olivia asks Viola in *Twelfth Night* what she thinks of her face, or when Claudius tells Hamlet he regards him as a son, what are Olivia's or Claudius' unconscious thoughts?

- What will Hamlet *do* physically when he says, "To be or not to be"? Will he move his arms? Will he stand still or move — and, if he moves, *where* is he moving to, and *why*, and *how*?
- When actors perform together, in pairs or groups, slightly different questions arise. What is Romeo thinking of when Juliet speaks to him from her balcony? How will the nuances of her performance affect Romeo? And how will the players achieve these effects?

On LEVEL 3, *we allow for the "filling in" that specific actors do*. We ask such questions as how would one actor play Romeo in the balcony scene in comparison with another? Or how would different actresses play Juliet in that scene? If the reader has little experience of "live" theatre, then comparisons of performers in film or television might be made — though they perform in a smaller, more intimate way than players on a stage, who act in a grander, larger manner. We might "cast" these performers as the people in the play as we read it.

Finally, we must ask the LEVEL 4 type of question. *What stage objects do the actors use, and how do these objects affect what happens?* Viola in *Twelfth Night* wears the costumes of a woman and of a man. These affect her movement: she can stride about in the male costume, but an Elizabethan bodice and skirt restrict her movements. When Launce enters in *Two Gentlemen of Verona* with his dog, Crab, is it a real dog, or is it imagined (like the rabbit in *Harvey*)? *What is done? Why is it done? And how is it done?* The answers will greatly affect the action of the play. In the Battle of Shrewsbury, Falstaff, a "gross, fat man," is a coward. When I played Falstaff in *1 Henry IV* (Leeds University, 1953; Colne Valley, 1959), I wore armour, a heavy helmet, a sword, a dagger, and heavy padding round my body. During the play I had to fall on the ground and act as if Falstaff were pretending to be dead. Later, I had to carry off the body of Hotspur, a big man also in armour. As an actor, I had to ask in both instances how Falstaff would do it and how it could be done. Such questions illustrate the practical nature of the plays. These questions we do not ask of novels.

FINDING ARTISTIC MEANING

ACTORS OR CHARACTERS?

Too often, critics discuss the plays as if they were dealing *only* with real people and real events, as if they were happening in real life. Yet people and events change with the actors who are playing them. Here we face a major difficulty: *looked at practically, stage roles are actors, but looked at artistically, stage roles are people.* When we read a play we should look at roles in both ways. Unlike novels, plays are simultaneously both practical events and works of art.

Are some dimensions more important than others? This problem was faced by Shakespeare in the late 1590s when the leading comic actor, Will Kempe, left the company and was replaced by Robert Armin. Shakespeare could no longer write the type of part he had created for the quick-witted Kempe, when the role was to be played by the slower Armin. His plays had to be changed. But what happened when the King's Men revived a play in which Kempe had created the role? Armin now had to act it, and the dramatic events changed practically and artistically. A Shakespearean play is always new on stage. With new actors, we in the audience have a different experience from the one we had with other actors.

Readers, like actors and audience, approach the people within a play in two stages: *we go THROUGH the actor to the role, and THROUGH the role to the person.* That is to say, when acting Macbeth about to murder Duncan, the actor asks *what* does Macbeth do? *Why?* And *how?* Will he see a real dagger, or will he imagine it? He has to settle these questions as himself, the actor; as himself in role; and artistically as Macbeth. Similarly in comedy, the actress playing Portia in *The Merchant of Venice* dresses as a male lawyer to defend Antonio in court. At each step in the scene, the actress must ask of Portia *what* she does, *why*, and *how.* The answers to such questions throughout the play make up the total person of Macbeth or Portia.

Readers must also "discover" a text both technically *and* artistically. If you read *The Taming of the Shrew*, you will have to ask the questions I asked when playing Christopher Sly: What does the *actor-in-role* do? (He stays on the chair in which he has been placed.) Why? (Because the Lord is playing a trick on him.) How? (With eyes open as if in a daydream, slurred speech, drunken gestures.) What does the *person* do? (He thinks he dreams.) Why? (He's drunk.) How? (With bewilderment and pleasure.)

POETIC, IMAGINATIVE, AND SYMBOLIC MEANING

Why are Shakespeare's plays so important to humanity? They convey enormous meaning. *King Lear* is not just about an old king who stupidly gives away his kingdom to two of his three daughters, who treat him so badly that he goes mad and dies. That is the broad storyline, which sounds almost like a "soap opera." But there is much more to the play.

First, much of it is in verse. Prose conveys ordinary meaning, but poetry gives us *extra*ordinary meaning. In *King Lear* the old king, turned out of doors by his ungrateful daughters, is caught in a raging storm. If he were going to convey ordinary meaning, he might say:

> Listen to that thunder, and that awful wind. It's raining so hard that the churches will get wet, and many chickens and cockerels will drown.

But he does not. What he says is:

> Blow, winds, and crack your cheeks! Rage! Blow!
> You cataracts and hurricanoes, spout
> Till you have drenched the steeples, drowned the cocks!
> (III.ii.1-3)

Say that aloud as if you are shouting at the storm (with no pause between "spout" and "Till"). Now that is *not* ordinary! Nor is it "natural"; kings in ancient Britain did not talk like that. Shakespeare takes the language to a new and higher level and gives it richer and more complex meanings.

Poetry helps Shakespeare to expand his imaginative ideas. What Lear says to his daughter, Regan, when she turns against him, is:

> You nimble lightnings, dart your blinding flames
> Into her scornful eyes! Infect her beauty,
> You fen-sucked fogs drawn by the powerful sun
> To fall and blister. (II.iv.160-163)

Say that, spitting it out in fury and contempt (with no pause between "flames" and "Into"). Now *that* is how to curse! Look at the images Shakespeare uses. "You fen-sucked fogs" has fogs being sucked up from wet fenland by the sun. You can only speak that phrase clearly by emphasizing the "ked" at the end of "sucked" with the "d" as a "t" (thus, "suck't"). Try it once more. Remember the lightning flames blinding Regan's eyes, infecting her beauty and blistering her. It sounds harsh and bitter.

Shakespeare also gives us imaginative meanings: the great storm that buffets Lear is also the storm of life we all must face. It destroys him. How can we stop it from destroying us? His daughters have been warped by the power of kingship, symbolized as a crown. Often to Shakespeare, "crown" signifies temporal power, contrasted with love for others and humanity as a whole. Such ideas extend our thoughts beyond the mere words.

WHAT IS REALISM IN SHAKESPEARE?

The people and the events of a Shakespearean play are *not* "real life." They are dramatic fictions. Yet Shakespeare's works are "life-like," or "true to life." No other dramatist gives us such an accurate picture of human life. But it is a "picture," *not the reality of life itself,* that occurs within the nature and conditions of the stage. This is the kind of experience we try to capture when we read a Shakespearean play. It is grander and more profound than the so-called "reality" of television. Each drama creates a *play world* of its own.

WHAT IS SAID AND DONE

When we read a play by Shakespeare, we create our own reality: we compare the practical with the imaginative. We read the words on the page in two ways, and our comparisons make the script "live" in our minds.

But one particular danger we must notice: *what is said* (the words on the page) does not always easily reveal *what is done.* The reader must treat the script like a detective story: hidden within the text are many clues about *what is done* on the stage. Sometimes the solution is easy, like most stage directions. *Enter Hamlet* is quite simple, except that we must ask *why? Where?* And *how?* But *Exit pursued by a bear* is not as simple as it seems. When we reach the stage implications of the dialogue, sometimes the problem would daunt the most brilliant sleuth. When the old, fat Falstaff is teasing Bardolph about his huge red nose:

BARDOLPH: 'Sblood, I would my face were in your belly!

FALSTAFF: God-a-mercy! So should I be sure to be heart-burnt.

Enter Hostess.

FALSTAFF: How now, Dame Partlett the hen!

(1 Henry IV, III.iii.48-51)

Why does Falstaff call the Hostess "Dame Partlett the hen," when her name is Mistress Quickly, and there is no other mention of chickens? Is this a hint that her laughter as she enters sounds like a hen's cackle?

When the shrew Katherine is wooed by the brash Petruchio:

KATH: I knew you at the first
You were a movable.

PET: Why, what's a movable?

KATH: A joint stool.

PET: Thou hast hit it. Come, sit on me.

(The Shrew, II.i.196-198)

What acts does Shakespeare imply here? Much will depend on the players, but Katherine could thrust him away on "movable" so that he sits suddenly on a stool and then pulls her onto his knee with "come sit on me."

As another example, on the battlefield, Lear carries in the dead Cordelia and puts her down:

LEAR: Lend me a looking-glass;
If that her breath will mist or stain the stone,
Why then she lives....
This feather stirs; she lives!

(King Lear, V.iii.259-263)

To see if a person was still breathing, Elizabethans used mist on a mirror or the movement of a feather. Even if someone finds a mirror for Lear on a battlefield, where does the feather come from? Probably from nowhere. The others know Cordelia is dead and give Lear nothing. In his distress, Lear imagines both mirror and feather.

KINDS OF REALITY

Shakespeare knew two kinds of reality. One was the reality of Renaissance England in which apprentices, burghers, and aristocrats were an audience watching a play. They lived in a world of ordinary experience: the *actual world*. Reality was what everyone with common sense knew it to be, and those who did not were dreaming or were "mad."

But within that ordinary, commonsense reality was another: the *play world*. Similar to the "world" of the child at play, which children believe to be as "real" as the everyday, the *play world* on a stage that Shakespeare's audience knew was not actual, not "real" as the world they lived in was real. But a play performed on a stage might *appear* to be real. Then the actors were not actors but flesh and blood persons who laughed and cried like people in the actual world. The reality of the *play world* was imaginative: created in the mind of the playwright, the actors, and the audience together. When Jaques in *As You Like It* says, "All the world's a stage," Shakespeare compares the two realities in a double metaphor: life is like a theatre, and theatre is like life. And this is the metaphor Shakespeare uses throughout his plays.

But the Renaissance audience was not *quite* sure of the difference. They did not, for example, clearly separate the actual (the natural) from the *supe*rnatural, nor the supernatural from the dream. Thus at the end of his life, Shakespeare creates for Prospero the lines:

> We are such stuff
> As dreams are made on. 　　*(The Tempest,* IV.i.156-157)

Here, it is not that life is like theatre, or that theatre is like life, but that life *is* a play, and that people are created from such dreams.

The complication comes when we, today, are part of an audience for one of Shakespeare's plays. If there were two realities in Shakespeare's time, the ordinary Renaissance actuality and the *play world* of, say, *Hamlet* on the stage, are we in a modern audience, then, another reality? And what reality does the reader have?

You, the reader, must answer that for yourself ...

THE EARLY HISTORY PLAYS

PLAYS OF WAR

I t is always exciting to read the first attempts of a great dramatist even if they are about a world of war. We do not know if Shakespeare created histories or comedies first, but of his early history plays, five are set in England and one in ancient Rome. All have a tragic tone. They are full of warfare and weeping, violence and victories, and Shakespeare's first major characters emerge in spell-binding scenes.

Four plays tell about the Wars of the Roses *(King Henry VI, Parts 1, 2 and 3,* and *King Richard III),* one is about medieval times *(King John),* and the Roman drama is *Titus Andronicus.* The latter is a very early play: lurid and violent, it is weak compared with Shakespeare's other plays, particularly *Richard III,* which is his first masterpiece.

Tudor interest in King John was religious. He was the only medieval English king to defy the Pope. To Catholics he was a heretic, but to Protestants he was a hero. Henry VIII and Elizabeth I brought about the Protestant Reformation, which Catholics wanted to reverse. Spain tried to do so with the Armada, defeated in 1588. It was about this time that Shakespeare arrived in London, and the city was full of stories about Catholic plots.

All these plays were written in the late 1580s or early 1590s, a time of exciting events. Plays about English history, which commented on present events and sometimes on particular people, were very popular. The English populace worried because Queen Elizabeth I was aging. When she died, would the new sovereign be able to control the realm? Shakespeare used previous civil wars to illustrate questions that were talked about by his contemporaries. That he did so in such a thrilling manner, and with such control over the theatre, despite his youth, demonstrates his remarkable ability.

Of these early histories, only *Richard III* contains echoes of the Providence found in the chroniclers [see *End Notes*]. To this Shakespeare adds the tradition of Richard the Devil, the deformed Crookback as a Senecan tyrant, and converts him into one who "turns the world upside down": a unique, ruthless, demonic comedian with a seductive appeal — the reverse of Christian sentiment. By this conflict of myths, Shakespeare constantly inverts meanings, words and word-patterns, roles, dramatic ironies, expectations, and moral values. He balances Christian retribution with historic irony. Of the paradoxes that result, he asks, "What is real?"

Later in his career, Shakespeare is conscious that "All the world's a stage" *(As You Like It,* II.vii.140). But in the *Henry VI* histories almost all of the play images are derivative: Suffolk's "To die by thee were but to die in jest" *(2 Henry VI,* III.ii.400) was a cliché used by Wyclif. What is extraordinary is that Shakespeare, from the beginning, uses so many of these images, taking advantage of the play metaphors inherent in the English language. He delights in words like "act," "scene," "tragedy," "perform," "part," and "play" which have both a non-dramatic and a theatrical meaning. He frequently uses the word "act" in the sense of deed or action, but rarely without some theatrical colouring. In performance these words remind the audience of the play-like nature of their own lives, and they lend an ominous quality to the stage.

"The weak king plays" of Shakespeare *(Henry VI, King John* and *Richard II)* and other dramatists were all written in a span of about ten years; they ask the questions most in people's minds at that time. They reveal the terrible effect of a weak king and the uncertainty about whether an inadequate monarch should be deposed. We are left with ambivalent feelings about the king: he is intended to be a consistent person, but our feelings about him shift sharply at different times. The Elizabethan audience was pulled two ways: between exasperation with an incompetent monarch and obedience to "God's deputy." One effect is that monsters are at large: York, Clifford, Cade, and Richard III destroy law and bring chaos; they are based on metaphors of moral conflict within the person, and they show the occasional inability of moral law to hold back human savagery.

The weak king plays are infused with Machiavellianism, which becomes "expediency" in England. This view is rejected by Shakespeare in *Henry VI* and shown in all its horror in *Richard III*. Later he tolerates the view in *Henry IV* and *Henry V* as a way to counter the despair created by a weak king. To "practical" politicians expediency meant that morality could be bent, and some committed atrocities for "political necessity." To audiences expediency meant the "stage Machiavel," an archvillain who was more appealing the craftier and bloodier he got, like Richard III. Only by using Machiavellian methods could a king succeed, yet for the ends to justify the means was immoral by Christian standards. Shakespeare combines the two moralities in the figure of Prince Hal in the *Henry IV* plays and *Henry V.*

Of Shakespeare's six early histories, one is a masterpiece: *Richard III*. One is a fascinating play which has never received its proper due: *King John.* Three are bitter chronicles of a weak king destroyed by Machiavels: *Henry VI, Parts 1, 2 and 3.* And one is a lurid melodrama: *Titus Andronicus.* The six histories are a remarkable beginning to Shakespeare's career as a dramatist.

THE *HENRY VI* TRILOGY

RE-DISCOVERING THE TRILOGY

𝕶 *ing Henry VI Parts 1, 2 and 3* have been subjected to a remarkable change of judgment. Fifty years ago they were thought poor plays, in which Shakespeare's hand was one among many. Today they are recognized, not as masterpieces, but as good strong plays that no one else could have written. How did this change occur?

These plays made the reputation of the young Shakespeare and were highly popular, as Henslowe's diary shows. They were certainly performed in the early 1590s, perhaps in the late 1580s. After several bad quartos, the trilogy was published in the 1623 *Folio,* and his colleagues, Hemmings and Condell, considered they were written by Shakespeare. But the plays fell out of favour in the theatre with the death of Queen Elizabeth I.

For centuries scholars dismissed the three plays, reluctant to attribute most of the trilogy to Shakespeare. "That Drum-and-Trumpet Thing," the eighteenth-century critic Maurice Morgann called it, "written doubtless, or rather exhibited, long before Shakespeare was born, tho' afterwards repaired, I think, and furbished up by him with here and there a little sentiment and diction."[*] For three hundred and fifty years, the *Henry VI* plays, especially in authentic rather than in drastically altered versions, appeared rarely on the stage.

Suddenly, in the 1950s, they were revalued. At the Birmingham Repertory Theatre from 1951 to 1953, and in 1953 at the Old Vic in London, Douglas Seale staged the whole

---

[*] For theatre history, see Ryan (1967) and Sprague (1964).

trilogy: *2 and 3 Henry VI* in 1951-52, and then *1 Henry VI* in 1953 in a cut version. It was a theatrical triumph, particularly for Jack May as Henry VI, Rosalind Boxall as Queen Margaret, and Edgar Wreford as both Dukes of Gloucester — Humphrey and Richard Crookback. For those of us who saw the production, Douglas Seale gave evidence that the trilogy was probably by Shakespeare.

In 1951-53, I directed sections of the trilogy in a series of *moro-spêches* (rehearsed readings with costumes and properties) with the Leeds Art Theatre Experimental Group. In working theatrically with the script I became convinced by its strength, structure, and characters that the trilogy was Shakespeare's. At about the same time, the Oregon Shakespearean Festival, at Ashland, began to stage the ten Shakespeare histories in the sequential order of the kings' reigns, one each summer.

Later, the trilogy was presented twice by the Royal Shakespeare Company at Stratford. In 1963-64, the *Henry VI* trilogy and *Richard III* were reworked as three plays, with many original textual additions by John Barton, called "The Wars of the Roses." In the 1977 production Terry Hands returned entirely to Shakespeare's text and played *Henry V* as an introduction to the *Henry VI* trilogy. His production confirmed the theatrical authority of the text of the trilogy as written. The plays have attracted great attention since, with many performances in Britain and internationally, showing not only that all three plays are far better than was once thought, but also that audiences thoroughly enjoy them.

Why were the plays unrecognized for so long? The plays are separate, with events that follow in sequence, and they probably include the earliest efforts of the young Shakespeare to create plays. Thus the poetry is not so memorable as in his masterworks, though there are sections of splendid verse. There are also resemblances in the text to the diction and verse of other Elizabethan dramatists, and, while this similarity might result from collaboration with others (as was thought in the past), it is probable that the young dramatist, just beginning his theatrical career, imitated other established playwrights.

Most of those who damned the plays were *literary* critics: their major criterion was the quality of the verse. Many of them, when the trilogy began to play to packed houses in the mid-twentieth century, thought it would be a flash in the pan. But it was not.

SHAKESPEARE AND HISTORY

In most Elizabethan chronicle plays we just observe the pageant of the past. In *Henry VI* we are forced to ask the meaning of humanity's role in history. Shakespeare's plays focus on the interaction of people within historical events and use an incredible mastery of construction, more observable in the theatre than in the reading. In his English histories we witness people's personal and social acts in the particular order allowed by God in the life of the realm. In the trilogy, the heroic Henry V is dead. His son, the gentle Henry VI, is no politician but a pious Christian: he values virtue and peace above power, and he uses one standard for personal and public conduct. At the core of the trilogy lies the issue of private and political morality. Evil people who ignore their proper place in the hierarchy drag everyone down into chaos. Hall says this is due to God's providence, but Shakespeare stresses human causes: the realm is torn by civil war when an unkingly king accepts all that happens to him as the will or justice of God. The *Henry VI* trilogy is a tragedy about a role that no one can fill. Henry VI tries to govern as a good Christian. He loves his fellow man and wants to do good in the world, but he is no match for the Machiavels. He is deceived, abused, deposed, and murdered. A monarch (throne or crown) to Shakespeare is an archetypal symbol, not a political idea. In the majesty of absolute power and the splendour of a crowned king, he embodies the health of the realm. Shakespeare develops this idea from play to play. Here, both king and realm are unhealthy.

In the years covered by the *Henry VI* trilogy (1422-61), there is tumultuous action: the stage is crowded with the hurly-burly of events and people. *Part 1* begins at the funeral of Henry V. The French have defeated the English because the political leaders jostle for power, leading to the vendetta of the houses of York and Lancaster. The Earl of Suffolk, who is married, falls in love with Margaret of Anjou; hoping to control the realm, he brings her home as Henry's bride.

Part 2 begins when Margaret arrives (1445) and ends with York's victory over Lancaster. It focuses on the downfall of Humphrey, Duke of Gloucester, who is caught in a plot of Margaret, Suffolk, and his old enemy Cardinal Beaufort.

Part 3 is a nightmare of unrelieved cruelty: the House of Lancaster, led by Henry and Margaret, struggles against the House of York, led by the Duke of York and his three sons. All but Henry have a lust for power. After many weary years of battles, the Yorkists win. Earlier, York himself had been ruthlessly murdered by Margaret and Clifford, so York's oldest son is crowned King Edward IV. Then Warwick changes sides, and Henry temporarily regains his throne. But in the end Edward is triumphant. Henry and his son are murdered by the bloody Richard Crookback.

Shakespeare shows the plight of people caught up in cataclysmic events, like so many in the world today; the prolonged violence breeds two figures who symbolize the political predicament of humanity — who shall be king? Henry or Richard, saint or sinner?

COUNTERFEITS

Counterfeits abound in both the *Henry VI* trilogy and *Richard III:* they are the Machiavels who practice *realpolitik* — false actors, every one. By working with the "scenes" and "acts" of death, Shakespeare uses the *theatrum mundi* [see *End Notes*] to re-create the plots of chronicle history. He creates them as if the people in history act the events like a play — not like life. That is, he *ritualizes* history: real actors play fictional people who are acting roles with others. When an important person falls from a high place, he or she also falls out of a role. Thus the fall of Joan la Pucelle in *1 Henry VI* is not only her capture and execution; she is also exposed as a fraud. Her presentation of herself as the "holy maid" (I.ii.51) is a false role which she loses. Each of these plays has (at least) three levels of illusion: real actors play characters, these characters play roles, and we in the audience watch them both. The *Henry VI* trilogy and *Richard III* possess *par excellence* the qualities of ritual and epic mimesis — and this gives them a basic power to move large audiences. They provide the Elizabethan spectators with a feeling of belonging to a heroic England ruled over by Elizabeth and recently reinforced by the defeat of the Spanish Armada. If the trilogy is more moving to watch than to read it is because it makes the historical facts theatrical.

HENRY VI, PART 1

FRICTION AND THE FEMININE

$\mathfrak{I}$n *1 Henry VI*, the youthful Shakespeare has arranged the chaotic mass of historical material into a masterly order. The whole play, the opening scene in particular, shows his powerful imagination and his control of both the dramatic and theatrical forms.

But it remains a youthful play with natural faults. The verse has enormous energy, but it does not make a great *poetic* drama. Some of Shakespeare's writing is similar to the dramatic idiom of the age. But none of his contemporaries is capable of such masterly structure or of the play's striking effect in the theatre. For a few details of the plot not in Hall and Holinshed, Shakespeare consulted the *Chronicles* of Robert Fabyan (1516) and Richard Grafton (1569), but many of the best scenes, such as the quarrel of the roses in the Temple Garden, he invented.

The characters are clear and consistent; at times they are pawns moved about the stage by an external hand, but almost all live and breathe, and there are some fine roles for actors to "fill in." Unlike the characters in Shakespeare's masterpieces, however, not everyone has a personal style of speech. But some have; Talbot, for example, has an elegiac tone. Characters may over-moralize or use over-ingenious rhetoric. Even so, *1 Henry VI* is strongly organized and packed with life.

THEMES
The important themes are vigorously, if a little roughly, realized in the theatre. There is no regular hero in the trilogy. England's hero, Henry V, is dead. Henry VI is buffeted by events and is not heroic. We identify with others, like Talbot, but their destinies are not the play's core. The true hero of the trilogy is England — the realm, the nation, the people — or *Respublica*, after the fashion of the morality play.

The central theme is the testing of England by French witchcraft, focused by Joan of Arc mainly at England's champion, Talbot. He might win and save England if the other English nobles were not divided against each other. So he dies. The first stage of England's ruin, and of God's curse after the overthrow of Richard II, is complete as the play ends.

Shakespeare shows the discord in the realm and its practical effects in two major ways. The nobles bicker and work against each other. Less obviously, but in a master stroke, Shakespeare presents three women whose sexuality threatens to overthrow English manhood: Joan, the Countess of Auvergne, and Margaret. The erosion of English virtue is brilliantly depicted in the triad of scenes in which each first appears: the manner in which the Dauphin, Talbot, and Suffolk respond to them simply dramatizes the lesson. Tudor woman is subservient to man in the cosmic order [see *End Notes*]; in a Shakespearean history play, politics and history are created by men, and men use deeds of courage, glory, patriotism, and honour to preserve their patriarchy. Paradoxically, Tudor women have no voice, and yet Elizabeth I reigns gloriously in England! Shakespeare is pulled both ways. He gives women a voice. All are French: the conflict of England vs. France becomes male vs. female values, chivalry vs. pragmatism, virtue vs. craft, age vs. youth, and high vs. low social rank. Talbot fights by chivalric rules, but Joan, a youthful peasant, uses craft and subterfuge. She recaptures Rouen by sneaking in to admit the French army. The Countess believes physical reality not verbal reports of it. She wants to confirm Talbot's glory in person ("Fain would mine eyes be witness with mine ears"), but what she sees ("a child, a silly dwarf") convinces her that the "report is fabulous and false" (II.iii.9-21). When Sir William Lucy describes the dead Talbot with his titles and military honours, Joan says:

> Him that thou magnifiest with all these titles
> Stinking and flyblown lies here at our feet.
>
> (IV.vii.75-76)

But this subversive female voice is only heard briefly; Shakespeare's audience will not permit more. For them, like the people in the play, Talbot's glory fills "the world with loud report," and his mere name is enough to rout the French sol-

diers (I.iv.50; II.i.79-81). The audience and the Countess want
to see the renowned Talbot, but both are disappointed. What
they see on stage is only a "shadow" of Talbot: male values are
protected against the feminine demand for physical facts
because the play is a fiction.

HISTORY AND FICTION

Shakespeare is cavalier with chronology. *1 Henry VI* disrupts the
time sequence more than any other of his history plays. But he
is not ignorant of history; his rearrangement of events shows
that he knows it well. He senses that dramatic logic is best
served by re-creating than by re-telling the past, and, unlike the
history plays of others, *1 Henry VI* clarifies the meaning of actual events.

Shakespeare also invents totally fictional scenes, among
them Talbot's meeting with the Countess of Auvergne, and juxtaposes events for striking dramatic and didactic effects. The
actual time span of the play is over thirty years (1422-1453). But
dramatic time is collapsed so that events that were actually
years apart are juxtaposed. Thus, for example, the siege of
Orleans (1428-29) coincides with the funeral of Henry V seven
years earlier, so that the main conflict between Joan-France and
Talbot-England can begin at once; to maintain this conflict as
long as possible, the death of the Talbots, which actually took
place much earlier, is put at the end of the play.

SYMMETRY AND STRUCTURE

Symmetry of design, as opposed to the formlessness of most
Elizabethan chronicle plays, is the structural focus of the trilogy
and of *Richard III*. There are many repeating dyads: parallel
and contrasting episodes, and confrontations of people who
represent different values. The action works at two levels: the
French fight to drive the English from their country; and the
English version of history and its values are attacked. Talbot
and Joan speak alternative languages: glory vs. physical objects,
English words vs. French things, and past vs. present. Dramatic
triads appear in many places from the opening scene onward:
the three messengers who urgently arrive one after another;
the three Frenchwomen; the trio of ambitious nobles

(Winchester, York, Suffolk); and the three loyal but aging generals (Salisbury, Bedford, and Talbot). Talbot opposes the French and Joan three times: at Orleans, where Salisbury is shot; at Rouen, where Bedford dies; and finally near Bordeaux, where he and his son meet their heroic end.

Shakespeare tells the story in two ways: as events and as rituals. Events are presented as if they actually happened, the people in them more alive and free. Rituals are symbolic actions: happenings with some higher significance, or turning-points in history, the people in them formal and symbolic. Thus Talbot's death is staged as a ritual: he represents the peak of English chivalry before it dies, the martial glory of England over France. When the English and French nobles meet over Talbot's corpse, the event (the harsh realities of the battlefield) and the ritual (a memorial tomb seen in the remote perspective of a later time) occur together. Talbot is discovered dead, with his son "inhearsèd in his arms," in tableaux fashion (IV.vii.45), like a figure on a monument. Indeed, Lucy's intonement of Talbot's titles comes from the inscription on Talbot's actual tomb at Rouen. Joan's reply answers the ritual by an event (IV.vii.75-77, as above). Shakespeare's use of ritual testifies to the continuity of his stage techniques with those of the tournament and the civic pageant, and to the continuity of the chronicles with play writing.

The linear structure switches back and forth from England to France; the story occurs in a double space. As with most Shakespearean plays, the act and scene divisions of later editors do not match the natural rhythm of the action which occurs in three Movements:

[1] the initial events in England and France (I.i-I.ii);

[2] the dissensions in England and the struggle between Talbot and Joan at Orleans, Rouen, Bordeaux — the main body of the play with the climax at Talbot's death (I.iii-IV.vii);

[3] Joan's burning, the King's marital confusions, and peace (V.i-V.v)

The alternations between England and France are deliberate on Shakespeare's part. Directors should not, like Osmond Tearle in 1889, stage the play so that Act I occurs in London and the other four acts take place in France!

ACTION

The First Movement: Introduction

As the court mourns Henry V there is dissension between the bad ambitious Beaufort, Bishop of Winchester, and the honest but hot-tempered Humphrey, Duke of Gloucester, Protector of the infant king. Bad news from France follows. Bedford goes to France; Humphrey takes charge at home (I.i).

It is the funeral of Henry V in 1422. A legendary warrior-king has just died. Muffled drums sound as the cortège slowly enters. In the solemn scene — "Hung be the heavens with black" — the king lies in state, symbol of the death of English heroism. The traditional final scene of a tragedy has become, with Shakespearean ingenuity, the opening scene here. The atmosphere is ominous; a sense of catastrophic loss mingles with fears for the future. The four funeral speeches by the king's brothers and uncles convey an awesome sense of cosmic upheaval and heavy finality. Men who later are bitter enemies join a chorus of praise mixed with lament:

> BEDFORD: Henry the Fifth, too famous to live long!
>   England ne'er lost a king of so much worth.
> HUMPH: England ne'er had a king until his time.   (6-8)
> BISHOP: He was a king blessed of the King of Kings. (28)

They unite in planning to crown the infant heir of Henry V as the new king — casually, as though no other succession is thinkable.

Dissension interrupts the funeral momentarily. It saps the English strength by the decay of feudal loyalties, an inversion of degree, a decline into French effeminacy, and the use of cunning rather than manly virtues. The struggle for power behind the throne between the Protector, Humphrey Duke of Gloucester, and the Bishop of Winchester spreads as others take selfish advantage of the confusion. Exeter says:

> What! shall we curse the planets of mishap
> That plotted thus our glory's overthrow?
> Or shall we think the subtle-witted French
> Conjurers and sorcerers, that, afraid of him,
> By magic verses have contrived his end?   (23-27)

Men dread the powerful influence of the stars and witchcraft.

Bedford's funeral invocation of Henry's ghost, to bless the realm and "keep it from civil broils" (line 53), is interrupted in mid-sentence by three messengers. They announce, in rapid succession, that several French cities have been retaken by the French, France has crowned the Dauphin king, and Lord Talbot, England's finest warrior, has been captured. The economy of the scene is shown in the impact of this trio of messengers: England has lost her moral superiority; the heroic past is overtaken by the present; and England's success in France depends on such leaders as Salisbury, Talbot, and Bedford. Shakespeare focuses on the three old warriors with heroic ideals, but they will soon be displaced by the Machiavels: the Winchesters, the Suffolks, and the Yorks.

What a superbly theatrical opening! The mastery of this scene is more evident in performance than in reading, because Shakespeare has learned his structural and performance skills before his poetic ones. With his love of symmetry, he ends the scene by repeating its opening pattern. The royal brothers and uncles take their leave in the same order in which they spoke. The effect in the theatre is magnetic: we briefly feel that, if they can work together, all may yet be well. But the rudderless realm is stressed in the pageantry of the departures, and, when all are gone, there remains the unscrupulous Winchester who sees his nephew's death as his opportunity to seize control "And sit at chiefest stern of public weal" (line 177).

> *Salisbury and the English occupy Orleans and drive the*
> *French back. Joan enters, fascinates Charles, the Dauphin,*
> *and beats him in single combat. She organizes the French,*
> *who agree to continue the battle (I.ii).*

Uniquely for Shakespeare, two scenes introduce the play; it has a double locale, England and France. The double movement of the battles (symmetrical attacks and counter-attacks) reflects the fickle movement of Mars, described by Holinshed. The Dauphin says:

> Mars his true moving, even as in the heavens
> So in the earth, to this day is not known.
> Late did he shine upon the English side;
> Now we are victors, upon us he smiles.   (1-4)

Charles is the exemplar of the low morality of Frenchmen. He is a braggart:

> Him I forgive my death that killeth me
> When he sees me go back one foot or fly. (20-21)

The French are ten men to one but are beaten back. The Dauphin says:

> I would ne'er have fled,
> But that they left me 'midst my enemies. (23-24)

Then Joan arrives and says: "Assigned am I to be the English scourge" (line 129). She dominates the Dauphin, beating him in single combat, and he woos her, not like her royal prince, but as a courtly lover. His response is scorned by the Tudor audience with its prejudice against Gallic effeminacy. The comedy of the double-entendre of lovemaking seen as armed combat leads the audience to dismiss Joan's claims to maintain her virginity and to have divine inspiration. When Charles cries,

> Bright star of Venus, fallen down on the earth,
> How may I reverently worship thee enough? (144-145)

the audience disbelieves Joan's pretensions and despises Charles's domination by a peasant. Shakespeare uses a Morality trick of turning a devil into a seeming angel; he shares the good and bad views of Joan credibly between French and English. Joan claims that her blonde beauty comes from the Virgin —

> And, whereas I was black and swart before,
> With those clear rays which she infused on me
> That beauty am I blessed with which you may see —
> (84-86)

but she really owes it to the Devil. She ends by imposing on the French a discipline and order which are unnatural to them. She symbolizes the soul of the rekindled war to the French, as Talbot does to England. With her appearance the fortunes of war turn from England to France; she rouses the French to enthusiastic patriotism by divine aid. Shakespeare does not deny this higher aid, but he sees it as coming from the Devil.

The Second Movement: Dissension and War

London: Winchester denies Humphrey entry to the Tower. They skirmish, and are separated by the Lord Mayor and officers (I.iii).

While the war continues in France, the play returns in four scenes to England. Shakespeare, like Holinshed, sees the English and French scenes as parallel: "Through dissension at home, all lost abroad." In my direction of the play, I focused the London scenes to stage right and the French scenes left, with contrasting lighting and banner colours. The action then swept on, scene to scene, in the Elizabethan manner.

In the Humphrey-Winchester feud, Shakespeare cleverly alters the formal reconciliation in the chronicle to a reluctant, casual handshake.

> *Orleans: Salisbury is killed and Talbot's men melt before Joan's attack. Though he is dauntless, she relieves the town. The French triumph. Bedford arrives with Burgundian allies, and together they retake the town (I.iv-II.ii).*

French cunning conspires with Mars to confound the English, as when the sniper shoots Salisbury from the "accursèd tower" (I.iv.76) — the upper stage *(tarras)*. Talbot (freed prior to this) suffers a setback because of Joan's "art and baleful sorcery." His martial skill and trust in God, in contrast with the Frenchmen's lax discipline and reliance on "the help of hell," win the day for him. "Coward of France!" exclaims Bedford of the Dauphin,

> how much he wrongs his fame,
> Despairing of his own arm's fortitude,
> To join with witches and the help of hell!   (II.i.16-18)

The full context of witchcraft is implied when Talbot says of the French:

> Well, let them practise and converse with spirits.
> God is our fortress, in whose conquering name
> Let us resolve to scale their flinty bulwarks.   (25-27)

These scenes in France contrast the behaviour of Joan, the Dauphin, and Englishmen who have also lost moral fibre with that of the upright Talbot. These contrasts are stressed by repeated patterns, including parallel episodes, and characters and events in triads.

> *Auvergne: the Countess tries to capture Talbot but fails (II.iii).*

There is a hint the Countess may have practiced sympathetic magic on her guest's portrait:

> Long time thy shadow hath been thrall to me,
> For in my gallery thy picture hangs;
> But now the substance shall endure the like.   (35-37)

The resourceful Talbot outwits her by a simple counterplot. He refuses, like a valiant knight, to avenge himself on so weak an adversary.

> *London, the Temple Gardens: the English lords quarrel;*
> *the Yorkists pluck white roses; the lords of Lancaster pluck*
> *red roses (II.iv).*

The scene is prophetic. A dispute has generated such fierce controversy that the lords have left the Temple Hall to carry their argument into the garden, and the legal issue ultimately gets lost.

> Great lords and gentlemen, what means this silence?
> Dare no man answer in a case of truth?   (1-2)

Plantagenet asks. Suffolk is indifferent to "truth" and law:

> Faith, I have been a truant in the law
> And never yet could frame my will to it;
> And therefore frame the law unto my will.   (7-9)

Feelings are intense as the two sides pluck the roses. When Plantagenet demands of Somerset, "Where is your argument?" (line 59) he replies,

> Here in my scabbard, meditating that
> Shall dye your white rose in a bloody red.   (60-61)

Somerset insults Plantagenet — "We grace the yeoman by conversing with him" (line 81) — the family title and lands were lost when Plantagenet's father was executed for treason by Henry V. The insult leads Plantagenet to find the truth; later, to a sense of injustice and his challenge for the crown.

Shakespeare invents the four London scenes to reveal the hidden bitterness in the dispute over the title to the throne. Plantagenet swears undying hatred toward his foes:

> And, by my soul, this pale and angry rose,
> As cognizance of my blood-drinking hate,
> Will I for ever, and my faction, wear
> Until it wither with me to my grave,
> Or flourish to the height of my degree.   (107-111)

Warwick makes the kind of prediction that is commonplace in

the histories:

> And here I prophesy: this brawl to-day
> Grown to this faction in the Temple garden,
> Shall send, between the red rose and the white
> A thousand souls to death and deadly night.   (124-127)

> *The Tower of London: Plantagenet's uncle, blind*
> *Mortimer, recites the history of his family and dies (II.v).*

Plantagenet learns the truth about his father by visiting his dying uncle. Edmund Mortimer, named by the childless Richard II as his heir, has been a lifelong prisoner of three Lancastrian kings. Blind and broken, he gives the Yorkist cause its initial thrust: he and his descendants were disinherited by Henry IV, and he exhorts Plantagenet to regain the title wrongfully held by the usurper's grandson. As Mortimer passes his frustrated ambition to his successor, he hints darkly at the possibilities:

> Thou art my heir. The rest I wish thee gather;
> But yet be wary in thy studious care.   (96-97)

To Plantagenet the execution of his father "was nothing less than bloody tyranny," but Mortimer advises caution:

> With silence, nephew, be thou politic.
> Strong fixèd is the house of Lancaster
> And like a mountain, not to be removed.   (101-103)

Mortimer embodies the futility of all such hopes. Emaciated, sightless and impotent after a lifetime in prison, he is "blind" to his own example. York is also "blind." Death ends Mortimer's exhausted hopes as Plantagenet says:

> Here dies the dusky torch of Mortimer,
> Choked with ambition of the meaner sort.   (122-123)

Plantagenet's own end at the hands of Clifford and Queen Margaret in *Part 3* will be even more ignominious.

> *The Parliament, London: before the young King Henry*
> *VI, the nobles quarrel and skirmish. Henry eventually gets*
> *them to stop and restores Plantagenet, making him Duke*
> *of York, annoying his rivals (III.i).*

We meet the youthful and innocent Henry VI for the first time. He enters to the full parliament with trumpets flourishing. The first major deceptions and betrayals occur among the lords. Henry makes a good beginning; he acts correctly. The two adversaries, Humphrey and the Bishop, angrily present their grievances, but the king rightly calls Winchester, not Humphrey, to account. The Bishop tells us, aside, that he is lying in agreeing to a reconciliation. The blot on the family's honour is removed, and Plantagenet is "restored to his blood"; he is made Duke of York by the King (line 162). Now York has a greater goal, the crown.

> *The pattern of Orleans is repeated at Rouen, France:*
> *Bedford dies, and through a trick Joan wins the town for*
> *the French. Again Talbot does not lose heart. He gets*
> *Burgundy to swear to capture the town or die. Unity once*
> *more succeeds. The town is recaptured by Talbot (III.ii).*

Talbot fights again, while Bedford watches the struggle from "his litter sick," insisting on taking his share of the battle:

> Here will I sit, before the walls of Rouen,
> And will be partner of your weal or woe.   (91-92)

Talbot emerges even more strongly as the symbol of true and virtuous order:

> Now will we take some order in the town,
> Placing therein some expert officers,
> And then depart to Paris to the King,
> For there young Henry with his nobles lie.   (126-129)

> *Between Rouen and Paris, Joan cheers the dispirited*
> *French leaders and says she has another plan. The English*
> *forces pass by; then the Burgundians, whom Joan waylays.*
> *She draws Burgundy from the English alliance (III.iii).*

This must have been a spectacular scene on the Elizabethan stage. The Dauphin, Joan, and the remnants of the French army enter (front stage). They watch as the English forces headed by Talbot pass across in triumph with colours spread, drums and trumpets playing, going to Paris (rear stage). The Burgundians follow, also ceremonially. Joan stops them, wins Burgundy to the French cause, and cynically says: "Done like a Frenchman — *[aside]* turn, and turn again." (line 85). On the unlocalized stage of the period, the scene requires many soldiers to have its true effect, even with speedy doubling. On a stage of the Fortune's size, with two doors, I found it necessary to have a minimum of five French, ten English and seven Burgundian soldiers (three were doubles) plus the speaking roles. All armies entered from the left door and exited by the right door. The French moved down front to let the English pass across; the three front English soldiers joined the rear of the Burgundians by a change of coloured tunic.

> *Henry VI's coronation in Paris: Talbot pays homage to him. Henry is crowned. At the news of Burgundy's defection, Talbot leaves at once. Yorkist and Lancastrian refer their quarrels to the King, who, not grasping the situation, frivolously chooses a red rose for himself and returns to England, leaving Somerset and York in divided command of the army, except the few that accompany Talbot (III.iv-IV.i).*

In another masterly construction, first Shakespeare presents us with a scene in an ante-room. Talbot's meeting with Henry VI is an idealized interview between an unselfishly devoted vassal and his sovereign. Talbot is created Earl of Shrewsbury, a parallel to Plantagenet's promotion to Duke of York. Having done nothing to merit it, Plantagenet, unlike Talbot, pledges his fealty to the king with a false heart (III.i).

The splendour of the coronation is interrupted by Burgundy's message. Vernon and Basset then further disrupt the ceremony with their demands for trial by combat on behalf of their respective masters, York and Somerset. Their two scenes (III.iv; IV.i) extend the dispute to the servants. York and Somerset conduct their quarrel according to "the law of arms," while the lower orders do not.

Henry's true stroke of political genius in *1 Henry VI* is also his biggest mistake: he puts on a red rose to indicate the folly of the contention in his kingdom. His forthright gesture and freedom from subterfuge shows the deceit of the lords:

> I see no reason, if I wear this rose, *[He puts on a red rose]*
> That anyone should therefore be suspicious
> I more incline to Somerset than York;
> Both are my kinsmen, and I love them both.
> As well they may upbraid me with my crown
> Because, forsooth, the King of Scots is crowned.

But your discretions better can persuade
Than I am able to instruct or teach .... (IV.i.152-159)

The lords are already so deep into "seeming" and *realpolitik* that, despite Henry's leadership, no one is listening.

> *Bordeaux: Talbot and his son are killed in battle with the French because York and Somerset refuse to send him forces (IV.ii-IV.vii).*

As Talbot has no support from the English lords, Joan does not need to use witchcraft to gain advantage over him. Sir William Lucy appeals to York and Somerset to send Talbot arms:

The fraud of England, not the force of France,
Hath now entrapped the noble-minded Talbot.
Never to England shall he bear his life,
But dies betrayed to fortune by your strife. (IV.iv.36-37)

They do not send arms, and Talbot, though he does all he can, perishes on heaps of French dead. Lucy recites Talbot's great titles, at which point Joan says:

Him that thou magnifiest with all these titles
Stinking and flyblown lies here at our feet. (IV.vii.75-76)

English idealism has fallen to French realism.

The Third Movement: Preparing for Marriage and Peace

> *In London, Humphrey suggests the King's marriage to the daughter of the Earl of Armagnac, and Winchester (now Cardinal) goes to France to arrange peace (V.i).*

> *Near Anjou, Joan's evil spirits desert her, and she is captured by York and burnt. Suffolk captures Margaret of Anjou and (wanting her as his mistress) arranges with her father, Reignier, for her to marry Henry VI. The Cardinal arranges a peace with the French (V.ii-V.iv).*

Contrary to history, but with excellent dramatic sense, York is made Joan's captor and judge. The parting curses of Joan are not the impotent ragings of a "fell banning hag" but prophesy the downfall of York and the miserable years for England due to Suffolk and Margaret. Joan ceases to be God's tool, loses her power, her evil spirits leave, and she is burnt. Are we meant to think that her evil spells are transferred to Margaret of Anjou? The meeting of Suffolk and Margaret, Reignier's daughter, shows that Englishmen no longer are men of true honour. Suffolk is dazzled, almost bewitched, by Margaret's beauty. Having Joan and Margaret both captured in the same scene is a symbolic parallel which is theatrically effective; it rounds out the plot of *1 Henry VI* and anticipates *Parts 2 and 3*.

The patching up of a false peace, which holds no promise of a renewed civil order, prefigures the final loss of France. None of the many reconciliations has any goodwill, Shakespeare taking his tone from Holinshed.

> *In London, Suffolk persuades the King to marry Margaret rather than the daughter of the Earl of Armagnac, suggested by Humphrey (V.v).*

The Earl of Suffolk (who is already married) falls in love with Margaret of Anjou and brings her home, without authorization, to be Henry's bride. Suffolk hopes to be her lover and to control the kingdom through her: such a betrayal of trust brings evil consequences in the chronicles. Henry, "too virtuous to rule the realm of England," is by nature non-passionate, but he is led by Suffolk's "wondrous rare description" of Margaret's beauty to break his pre-contract of marriage with his previous choice. The king's inner turmoil shows his decision to be impolitic and immoral. He compares his infatuation to a tempest, driving his soul like a ship against the tide:

> So I am driven by breath of her renown
> Either to suffer shipwreck or arrive
> Where I may have fruition of her love.   (7-9)

Most disturbing of all, however, are Suffolk's words at the end:

> As did the youthful Paris once to Greece,
> With hope to find the like event in love
> But prosper better than the Trojan did.   (104-106)

This image is not lost on an Elizabethan audience, whose own historians trace British ancestry to Troy. Margaret, like Helen, will bring disaster.

STRENGTH OR WEAKNESS?

Literary critics today acknowledge the strength of the structure and theatricality of *1 Henry VI* but tend to disparage the characterization and the writing. But are they, indeed, weak? Both are as strong as in the plays of Shakespeare's contemporaries, and, if they are not as fine as in his masterpieces, they have power. Shakespeare from the first knows that people use roles. England offers peace if the Dauphin will submit, but Alençon retorts:

> Must he be then as shadow of himself?
> Adorn his temples with a coronet,
> And yet, in substance and authority,
> Retain but privilege of a private man?
> This proffer is absurd and reasonless.   (V.iv.133-137)

Henry VI, however, has no role. He is very young, a "weak king," and a bad actor. Every person is consistent. The Machiavels are truly "false actors": Suffolk in the Temple Garden shows himself both diplomatic and unscrupulous; later he deals with Margaret, Reignier, and Henry in the same way. Plantagenet fully anticipates the "dogged York who reaches at the moon" in *Part 2*. Humphrey is good-hearted but outspoken to a fault and, with Talbot and the old warriors, honest and honourable. The Joan is that of the English chroniclers: she is a witch with her evil spirits and so is another kind of "false actor." She is a peasant and very down-to-earth, as she shows in her remarks on Burgundy's change of mind and over Talbot's dead body. The unsavoury side of her character is hinted at in her very first scene, and, while she is eloquent, efficient, and patriotic, she later reveals that her wantonness and diabolism were constant from the first. Some interpretations have not always realized this consistency: for example, the greatly abridged Old Vic version in 1923 gave Joan the same character as Shaw's *St. Joan*.

In places the writing is poor. Once or twice the rhythm is very lame, and sometimes there are lumps of turgid writing like that of the University Wits, who usually disparaged less-educated competitors like Shakespeare. But scattered through the play is some excellent poetry in Shakespeare's best style. Reignier, talking of the valour of English soldiers, uses the metaphor of an artificial man striking the hours of a clock with a hammer:

> I think by some odd gimmers or device
> Their arms are set like clocks, still to strike on;
> Else ne'er could they hold out so as they do. (I.ii.41-44)

Shakespeare uses this machine metaphor again with superb effect in *Richard III*. Talbot, offering terms to the French commanders in Bordeaux, can reach grandeur:

> But, if you frown upon this proffer'd peace,
> You tempt the fury of my three attendants,
> Lean famine, quartering steel, and climbing fire;
> Who in a moment even with the earth
> Shall lay your stately and air-braving towers,
> If you forsake the offer of their love.   (IV.ii.9-14)

The play has vehement energy, revealed in performance, and a tough and resilient structure. This single play is conceived as an organic part of a vast design; for a young dramatist, Shakespeare shows extraordinary bravery. History plays rely on ceremony. Shakespeare in this play uses three — and *interrupts* them! The funeral of Henry V, the proceedings at Parliament House, and the coronation of Henry VI have spectacular pageantry and music. For other dramatists, that would be enough. But for this young man, scarcely out of his teens, it is not. He realizes that the ritual pageantry and slow drumbeat of a great hero's funeral can be tightened up to greater tension through interruption. So he has three messengers arrive one after the other. The effect of this invention can only be discovered in the theatre, not in the reading. It is so successful that he interrupts two other ritual ceremonies. Too much of a good thing, perhaps? He would discover this with the audience present, and we can see the results in his even greater plays.

HENRY VI, PART 2

THE FALL OF GREAT MEN

Henry VI Part 2 may be Shakespeare's first dramatic work. The play centers on the fall of Humphrey, Duke of Gloucester, the Lord Protector and uncle of the king. He falls foul of the Machiavels, is murdered, and the result is political chaos. The king is a paradox: he possesses the crown but wants to be a commoner.

> Was never subject longed to be a king
> As I do long and wish to be a subject.   (IV.ix.5-6)

Yet many of his subjects plot to be king. The attitude of these stage Machiavels to Humphrey and Christian morality is consciously false: they are hypocrites. Lusting for power, they use any deceit to get it. All assume moral roles but are false actors. They breed dissension, paralyze action at court and overwhelm society. When Humphrey falls, chaos results — the punishment for the sin of Richard II's murder [see *End Notes*]. But the Machiavels blame the chaos on the weak king. Some modern critics agree, but Shakespeare sees the Machiavels as evil and politically ineffective. This is clear in the theatre: after the 1953 Seale production, most players see Henry in *Part 1* as a young man following his Protector's advice, and in *Part 2* as a good Christian, engulfed by evil.

BACKGROUND TO THE PLAY

Parts 2 and 3 were certainly written and performed earlier than June 23, 1592. Probably they were originally a two-part play, and *Part 1* came later. The publication of the second edition of Holinshed's *Chronicles* (1587) may provide the earliest date limit. Shakespeare's main source is the chroniclers for whom chaos comes from sin; Shakespeare combines this idea with the

Machiavellian belief that chaos comes from weakness [see *End Notes*].

In dramatizing history, Shakespeare has many problems:

[1]   The plot is a given.

[2]   He must shape the story, select detail, and impute motives.

[3]   Limited by sources, historical "facts," and the need not to offend the powers-that-be, he must compress time and change the order of events: twenty years of the Lancaster-York struggle is one sequence of events.

[4]   Restricted to a small cast, he must make pairs of antagonists (or events) symbolic: the York-Old Clifford duel becomes false vs. loyal nobility.

[5]   He must increase continuity by stressing some non-facts: only Shakespeare links Cade's uprising to York.

[6]   He must make a slice of historical time seem complete and self-contained: York rises from a strong, silent rival claimant using the ironic aside and soliloquy (I.i; III.i), to an enemy loudly defying the king. Parallel is King Henry's slide into helplessness and despair:

Come wife, let's in, and learn to govern better;
For yet may England curse my wretched reign.

(IV.ix.48-49)

Attitudes to *2 Henry VI* have changed over time. A major revision by John Crowne was produced about 1681 with Mr. and Mrs. Betterton as Humphrey and Eleanor. Ambrose Phillips's *Humfrey Duke of Gloucester* (1723) owes little to Shakespeare. Edmund Kean as York, with Munden as Cade, acted most of the play at Drury Lane in 1817; and it was played in London in 1864 when James Anderson doubled York and Cade. Sir Barry Jackson wrote that of the Shakespearean history plays produced at Stratford-upon-Avon by F. R. Benson in 1906, "it was the unknown *Second Part* of *King Henry VI* that made the greatest impression on my mind."* About this time, Arthur Machen and Matheson Lang were notable as the Conjurer. Of modern productions, that of Douglas Seale was

---

* Jackson (1953).

the most impressive although the Cade scenes were disappointing (1953); but Esmond Knight was a memorable Cade in Peter
Dews' BBC TV "Age of Kings" series (1960). The greatest
Margaret of our time was Barbara Jefford at the Old Vic
(1957).*

STRUCTURE

The structure is unique because the play is assumed to begin
and end in other plays. Yet *Part 2* has its own design in which
Shakespeare uses less heraldry and pageantry than in *Part 1,*
and increases his use of the techniques of the Morality play and
of Seneca.

The natural movement of the dramatic action in *2 Henry VI*
is initiated by the marriage of King Henry and Margaret of
Anjou. The movement then follows in one continuous sweep
that has little relation to the act and scene divisions of later editors. To the chroniclers and Shakespeare, the unseen back-
ground of Henry VI's reign is France. In the person of
Margaret, and the bickering of the English lords, France is the
context of all the failures in the play. The loss of England's
French possessions parallels the loss of English loyalty. France
and Queen Margaret are the Senecan curse that lurks behind
the action. The movement forward has two waves:

[1]   The Primary Wave
The emotional structure is based in two crises: the
play climbs to the martyrdom of Humphrey in Act III,
where the strongest moral-political positives occur,
and it falls to the end, where the battle provides the
most powerful negative statements. In this latter part,
Humphrey's murder is replayed in another form: it
becomes a model of the social and political turmoil.
What is ended is Humphrey's political belief in the
human capacity to serve God by independent moral
strength and intelligence. He stands for the fealty and
dedication to the crown of medieval times, but the
other lords are all Renaissance Machiavels. Thus his
death in the play is inevitable.

---

* For stage history, see Ryan (1967) and Sprague (1964).

[2]   <u>The Second Wave</u>
      Within the major structure lies a second wave.
This is the rhythmic pattern of related playlets: men
fall, as in medieval "tragedies," and this decline is a
sub-structure for the trilogy and *Richard III*. In *2
Henry VI* these playlets are near the surface and operate as successive waves: one villain falls, and another
replaces him — Eleanor, Humphrey, Suffolk, Lord
Say, Somerset. Each is accused, arrested and killed
until, at the end, King Henry confronts the raw malice of York. Each performs a playlet, a kind of "play
within a play." The first is that of Humphrey's wife,
Eleanor, who sees her playlet as "Fortune's pageant";
the actor eagerly seeks to play his part (I.ii.66), but
the playlet grows into the "plotted tragedy" of
Humphrey's lament (III.i.153). Hers is the prototype
for the rest. She cannot persuade her good husband
to usurp the crown, so she echoes York's resolve to
find some way of getting rid of "these tedious stum-
bling-blocks" (I.ii.64). She already imitates the role of
queen, as Margaret sneers (I.iii.75-77), so she now
tries to genuinely act the role: she dabbles in black
magic, gets caught, is sentenced to banishment, and
must undergo public penance (II.iv). She loses the
role she held, she fails to gain the role she wanted,
and she is forced to play an unwanted role, with its
costume and trappings — she enters barefoot, a white
sheet about her, a wax candle in her hand, and verses
pinned to her back. She cannot endure her present
shame, so she longs for no role at all — "Ah,
Gloucester, teach me to forget myself" (II.iv.27).

The play has four Movements: [1] Setting the Context, [2] The
Fall of Eleanor and Humphrey, [3] Retribution and the Cade
Revolt, and [4] the Rise of York.

ACTION

The First Movement: Setting the Context

Margaret of Anjou is welcomed as queen. Suffolk has married her in France as the King's proxy. In the marriage agreement England loses Anjou and Maine; Humphrey is furious (I.i).

No sooner is there a *Flourish of Trumpets: Then hautboys* announcing the arrival of Margaret than she and Humphrey struggle for control of the gentle king. Humphrey addresses the assembled lords:

> O peers of England, shameful is this league,
> Fatal this marriage, cancelling your fame,
> Blotting your names from books of memory,
> Razing the characters of your renown,
> Defacing monuments of conquered France,
> Undoing all, as all had never been!   (96-101)

Humphrey symbolizes the law and the integrity of the people. Animal images cluster to him: a victimized heifer or partridge (by Warwick), an unweaned calf (by Henry), or a shepherd to the lamb-king (by Humphrey). The executor of the law, he is also its victim. His honesty brings enemies: the Cardinal (the Church) from *Part 1*; Margaret and her lover, Suffolk, as the loss of Anjou and Maine was caused by the marriage; and Somerset and Buckingham —

> SOM: Cousin of Buckingham, though Humphrey's pride
> And greatness of his place be grief to us,
> Yet let us watch the haughty Cardinal;
> His insolence is more intolerable
> Than all the princes' in the land beside.
> If Gloucester be displaced, he'll be Protector.
> BUCK: Or thou or I, Somerset, will be Protector,
> Despite Duke Humphrey or the Cardinal.
>   (170-177)

Somerset's "let us watch" is spoken by a Machiavel. York seems to support Humphrey (line 242), but he switches sides after Humphrey's imprisonment. He sees himself as the true king watching the usurper give away the realm. He

> Weeps over them, and wrings his hapless hands,
> And shakes his head, and trembling stands aloof,
> While all is shared and all is borne away,
> Ready to starve, and dare not touch his own.   (224-227)

In his view, Henry holds "the sceptre in his childish fist" (line 243), while his "church-like humours fits not for a crown" (line 245). York is resolute:

> And force perforce I'll make him yield the crown,
> Whose bookish rule hath pulled fair England down.
>
> (256-257)

The Second Movement: The Fall of Eleanor and Humphrey

> *Humphrey's wife, Eleanor, resorts to black magic with*
> *Hume, a conspirator for Suffolk and the Cardinal (I.ii).*

> *Margaret and Suffolk deal with petitioners to the Protector.*
> *Humphrey is demeaned; Margaret boxes Eleanor's ears.*
> *Humphrey makes Somerset regent over France (I.iii).*

Not only York thinks badly of Henry. His wife compares him to Suffolk:

> I thought King Henry had resembled thee
> In courage, courtship, and proportion.
> But all his mind is bent to holiness,
> To number Ave-Maries on his beads;
> His champions are the prophets and apostles,
> His weapons holy saws of sacred writ;
> His study is his tilt-yard, and his loves
> Are brazen images of canonized saints.
> I would the College of the Cardinals
> Would choose him Pope, and carry him to Rome,
> And set the triple crown upon his head -
> That were a state fit for his holiness.   (I.iii.51-62)

Suffolk and Margaret plot against Humphrey. He replaces York by Somerset in France: "This is the Law, and this Duke Humphrey's doom" (line 208).

> *The conjuring scene before Eleanor. York and Buckingham*
> *break in and arrest the participants (I.iv).*

> *The court is falconing but quarrels break out. A blind*
> *man of St. Albans (Simpcox) claims a miracle as he can*
> *now see, but Humphrey shows him to be an imposter (II.i).*

The conjuring scene is a piece of stage sensation, loved in
the nineteenth century. Lady Benson thought it excellent on
the stage (1906).*

Henry has to admonish his attendant nobles and the Queen:

> I prithee peace,
> Good Queen, and whet not on these furious peers;
> For blessèd are the peacemakers on earth.   (II.i.32-34)

Henry believes the false miracle, saying "Now God be praised."
Humphrey, a good judge, shows Simpcox is an impostor and
Henry says: "O God, seest thou this, and bearest so long?" (line
150). Margaret comments harshly, "It made me laugh to see
the villain run" (line 151). In the comic Simpcox scene,
Humphrey, "beloved of the commons," cleverly improvises
practical justice. Shakespeare casts Humphrey in Morality
terms but tempers this role with humanity: Humphrey speaks
of his Duchess in tones poised between personal feeling and
the decorum of his office (line 189).

> *York persuades Warwick and Salisbury to his cause (II.ii).*

York plots to allow the rest ("all the crew of them") to
destroy Humphrey and, when the wolves have "snared the
shepherd of the flock," to move against the King (lines 69-73).
York is not without persuasive power:

> What plain proceedings is more plain than this?
> Henry doth claim the crown from John of Gaunt,
> The fourth son; York claims it from the third.
> Till Lionel's issue fails, his should not reign;
> It fails not yet, but flourishes in thee,
> And in thy sons, fair slips of such a stock.   (53-58)

Warwick and Salisbury kneel to York as their true and legal king.

> *The king banishes Eleanor to the Isle of Man and dis-*
> *misses Humphrey as Protector. Peter kills the Armourer*
> *(Horner) in a ritual combat while drunk (II.iii).*

---

* See Sprague (1964).

Humphrey watches Eleanor's penance (II.iv).
Eleanor's humiliation pictures the cruelty of

> The abject people gazing on thy face,
> With envious looks, laughing at thy shame   (II.iv.11)

which steadily enlarges into a threnody with medieval echoes; it includes the conventional image of summer giving way to barren winter, and the sentiment about the irony of personal misfortune — "To think upon my pomp shall be my hell" (line 41).

> *The Queen and lords talk against Humphrey; the King
> defends him. News arrives: England has lost all France.
> Humphrey is arrested, and the King exits in tears.
> Margaret, Suffolk, York, and the Cardinal agree
> Humphrey should be killed. York will subdue Ireland (and
> plans Cade's revolt) (III.i).*

This scene is superbly constructed. Henry cannot control his court or his realm. The Queen tries to poison Henry's mind against Humphrey:

> Small curs are not regarded when they grin,
> But great men tremble when the lion roars;
> And Humphrey is no little man in England.
> First note that he is near you in descent,
> And should you fall, he is the next will mount.   (18-22)

Henry will not believe him guilty:

> but, shall I speak my conscience,
> Our kinsman Gloucester is as innocent
> From meaning treason to our royal person
> As is the sucking lamb or harmless dove.   (68-71)

Yet he cannot save him. After the formal charges, Henry says:

> My Lord of Gloucester, 'tis my special hope
> That you will clear yourself from all suspense;
> My conscience tells me you are innocent.   (139-141)

Henry is not guilty of inaction; he relies on the legal system of the land and his own belief that right will triumph. But he has a rude shock. His inability to protect Humphrey is more than a humiliating failure to secure justice; it also makes Henry vulnerable to York's plans. Humphrey says:

> Ah, gracious lord, these days are dangerous;
> Virtue is choked with foul ambition,
> And charity chased hence by rancour's hand;

Foul subornation is predominant
And equity exiled your highness' land.   (142-146)
Humphrey also sees his own death at his enemies' hands as a
beginning:

mine is made the prologue to their play;
For thousands more, that yet suspect no peril,
Will not conclude their plotted tragedy ...   (151-153)

Humphrey's *agon* has a symbolic quality. But nothing can compel the king to act on his own. He even gives his power to those he mistrusts:

My lords, what to your wisdoms seemeth best
Do or undo, as if ourself were here.   (195-196)

The Queen is astonished: "What, will your Highness leave the parliament?" (line 197). Shakespeare ties the king's piety to Humphrey's integrity:

Ah, uncle Humphrey, in thy face I see
The map of honour, truth, and loyalty; ...
And as the butcher takes away the calf,
And binds the wretch, and beats it when it strays,
Bearing it to the bloody slaughter-house,
Even so, remorseless, have they borne him hence.
                                              (202-213)

Henry believes in Humphrey, but all he can do is to pour out his grief:

good Gloucester's case
With sad unhelpful tears, and with dimmed eyes
Look after him, and cannot do him good,
So mighty are his vowèd enemies.   (217-220)

When Henry goes, Margaret's comment to the nobles is contemptuous:

Henry my lord is cold in great affairs,
Too full of foolish pity.   (224-225)

Like Henry, the conspirators know a trial will prove Humphrey's innocence because they have "but trivial argument" (lines 231-243). They must murder him. This is the crisis of *Part 2* — it removes the only honest and strong person close to Henry. "Steel thy fearful thoughts," York says to himself,

Be that thou hopest to be, or what thou art
Resign to death; it is not worth th'enjoying.   (333-334)

For York, life is power. He ignores moral law. The crown is an all-consuming passion which he knows will destroy him because those who supply him with troops for Ireland have "put sharp weapons in a madman's hands" —

> This fell tempest shall not cease to rage
> Until the golden circuit on my head,
> Like to the glorious sun's transparent beams,
> Do calm the fury of this mad-bred flaw.   (351-354)

> *Before Humphrey can be tried, Suffolk has him killed.*
> *Warwick and Salisbury accuse Suffolk and the Cardinal*
> *of murder. Henry banishes Suffolk who parts with*
> *Margaret (III.ii).*

Henry opens the trial with a show of regal but futile firmness:

> Proceed no straiter 'gainst our uncle Gloucester
> Than from true evidence, of good esteem,
> He be approved in practice culpable.   (20-22)

When Humphrey's death is announced, Henry cannot believe it natural:

> O Thou that judgest all things, stay my thoughts,
> My thoughts that labour to persuade my soul
> Some violent hands were laid on Humphrey's life.
> If my suspect be false, forgive me, God,
> For judgement only doth belong to Thee.   (136-140)

Suffolk and Warwick counterfeit righteous indignation on either side. Then Henry speaks four highly significant lines:

> What stronger breastplate than a heart untainted!
> Thrice is he armed that hath his quarrel just,
> And he but naked, though locked up in steel,
> Whose conscience with injustice is corrupted. (232-235)

Too late, Henry acts — without law — and exiles Suffolk.

This whole event is a clever plot by York, now in Ireland. Henry plays a role in York's scenario. York and Warwick were part of the plot to kill Humphrey. When the murder occurs, Warwick is the first on the scene. Speaking for an enraged public (gathered in surprising haste) he accuses Suffolk. York and Warwick (better Machiavels than Margaret, Suffolk, and the Cardinal) reap the political benefit of the murder but none of the blame. York has planned events carefully; Humphrey's downfall leads directly to York's power grab.

This superb scene focuses on a theatrical metaphor, as

Humphrey's strangled body is exhibited. This staged device gives a spectacular force to a major theme, "Virtue is choked with foul ambition." To this stage action, Shakespeare adds a gripping verbal passage to emphasize the physical horror (lines 160-178). In front of the helpless king, the strangled body lies on the stage, while the Commons "like an angry hive of bees" (line 125) beat on the doors — they become the mob of Cade's rebellion. Margaret and Suffolk bid farewell (lines 300-412) in poetry of unusual tenderness. She says, "Even now be gone!" (line 352), kissing his hand, but:

> O, go not yet. Even thus two friends condemned
> Embrace, and kiss, and take ten thousand leaves,
> Loather a hundred times to part than die.   (353-355)

Suffolk's gentle response almost earns our forgiveness:

> 'Tis not the land I care for, wert thou thence;
> A wilderness is populous enough,
> So Suffolk had thy heavenly company;
> For where thou art, there is the world itself
> With every several pleasure in the world;
> And where thou art not, desolation.
> I can no more.   (359-365)

We have been unsympathetic to them, but our antagonism is shaken. There is nothing quite like this reversal in English plays before 1590. Shakespeare makes us suspend our judgment of them, to imagine events from their eyes. This is a radical piece of dramaturgy; Shakespeare learns from this innovation to create his later three-dimensional characters.

The Third Movement: Retribution and the Cade Revolt

The Cardinal on his deathbed confesses his complicity in Humphrey's murder (III.iii).

With Humphrey gone, the play shifts its tone. Humphrey says his death is but the prologue to the plotted tragedy, and for a generation atrocities are a routine of public life. Shakespeare's knowledge of Seneca helps him here. We observe what Foxe's *Book of Martyrs* called "the judgment of God upon them which persecuted the Duke."* The acts of retribution have a sickening

---

46 Bullough (1957-1975).

atmosphere of evil. The Cardinal, tormented by the ghost of Humphrey, dies in agony, while his enemy Warwick jeers, "See how the pangs of death do make him grin!" (line 24). Shakespeare presents the Cardinal's death with an implied causal chain of prophecy, omen, and curse, repeating the pitiless pageant of Providence in Holinshed and Foxe.

In a fight at sea, Suffolk is murdered (IV.i).

But Suffolk's death is a lynching, "a barbarous and bloody spectacle" (line 146) and not providential. Shakespeare's genius here lies in capturing the tragic rhythm of political history. Awaiting death at the hands of pirates, Suffolk has a new dignity. He refuses to humble himself before "these paltry, servile, abject drudges." (line 105):

> No, rather let my head
> Stoop to the block than these knees bow to any
> Save to the God of heaven, and to my king;
> And sooner dance upon a bloody pole
> Than stand uncovered to the vulgar groom.
> True nobility is exempt from fear. (126-131)

It is gruesome irony that Suffolk dies for God and King Henry.

Jack Cade declares a common realm. He confronts Sir Humphrey Stafford (IV.ii), who is slain. His armour is worn by Cade (IV.iii). Cade reaches London, and Henry flees (IV.iv). Lord Scales sends for men to defend the Tower (IV.v). Cade urges his men on (IV.vi). Lord Say addresses them and is killed (IV.vii). Buckingham and Old Clifford parlay, and the mob turns on Cade, who flees (IV.viii). Henry pardons Cade's men. York has arrived from Ireland. Henry imprisons Somerset (IV.ix). Iden kills Cade in his garden (IV.x).

Encouraged secretly by York, Cade poses as heir to the throne to lead the rabble in a revolt. The rebellion on stage, full of gallows humour, action, spectacle, and sociopolitical commentary, is very popular. Elizabethans saw history plays as analogues of the present. At that time, London was racked by riot, so these scenes were probably closely censored.

This Cade is not the audacious field general of Hall. He stands for terrifying ignorance. He executes a clerk because he can read and write, and Lord Say because of his cultural accomplishments. Say built a grammar school, so he "most traitorously corrupted the youth of the realm," surrounding himself with men "that usually talk of a noun and a verb, and such abominable words as no Christian ear can endure to hear" (IV.vii.29-37). Cade *is* anarchy and, in a ghastly way, is comic: "Away! Burn all the records of the realm; my mouth shall be the parliament of England" (lines 11-13); "There shall not a maid be married but she shall pay to me her maidenhead, ere they have it" (lines 113-115). When Cade says, "Then are we in order when we are most out of order" (IV.ii.179-180), he could be talking of the court. He claims a fanciful line of descent (IV.ii.123-137), in a ludicrous parody of the courtiers' genealogy.

The rebellion anticipates the great mob scenes in *Julius Caesar* and *Coriolanus*. It is a grim parody of York's pretentious rebellion. York says that Cade and his Kentishmen work on his behalf. Lord Say has Humphrey's role in the sense that his murderers are like the Machiavels (with a veneer of lower-class language and manners), and he is a Christian humanist:

> When have I aught exacted at your hands,
> But to maintain the King, the realm, and you?
> Large gifts have I bestowed on learnèd clerks
> Because my book preferred me to the King,
> And, seeing ignorance is the curse of God,
> Knowledge the wing wherewith we fly to Heaven,
> Unless you be possessed with devilish spirits,
> You cannot but forbear to murder me.   (IV.vii.64-71)

It is the humanist, with neither force nor guile, who most frightens the Machiavels. Always he is the first one they must dispose of.

Shakespeare distorts Holinshed to aid his own structure. The play's revolt is an evil consequence of Suffolk's acts: he and Margaret tear up the petitions of innocent citizens (I.iii.38), who become the apprentices of the Peter Thump scenes, the crowd at St. Albans, and the "mob" at Humphrey's death. Suffolk's actions force the people to take the law into their own hands. They are first free from a "stubborn opposite intent" (III.ii.251), but "thirsting after prey" (IV.iv.51) they are capable of atrocities.

The mob is finally won over by Buckingham and Clifford,

who restore their "order" (IV.viii) with a trumpet, and by the sight of two leading soldiers with their bodyguards. Henry's pardon, garbled by Buckingham (IV.viii.8), is lost in the peace. Buckingham and Clifford ask for allegiance in the name of "Henry the Fifth, that made all France to quake," and when the mob cries, "We'll follow Cade," it is checked with, "Is Cade the son of Henry the Fifth?" (IV.viii.15-16, 33-34). Cade sees the picture clearly: "Was ever feather so lightly blown to and fro as this multitude? The name of Henry the Fifth hales them to an hundred mischiefs and makes them leave me desolate" (IV.viii.54-57).

Cade has a splendid death scene. Deserted by the mob, he stumbles into the garden and is killed by Iden. As he dies, Cade evokes compassion:

> O, I am slain! Famine and no other hath slain me; let
> ten thousand devils come against me, and give me but
> the ten meals I have lost, and I'd defy them all.
>
> (IV.x.58-60)

The Fourth Movement: The Rise of York

> *York arrives with his army from Ireland. He is assured by*
> *Buckingham that Somerset is in the Tower, so York dis-*
> *misses his army. The King arrives, but Margaret brings*
> *Somerset. York is furious. The two sides square off (V.i).*

The atmosphere has changed. York returns, demanding his rights:

> From Ireland thus comes York to claim his right,
> And pluck the crown from feeble Henry's head.
> Ring bells, aloud; burn bonfires clear and bright,
> To entertain great England's lawful king.
> Ah, *sancta majestas!* Who would not buy thee dear?
> Let them obey that know not how to rule;
> This hand was made to handle naught but gold.   (1-7)

Retribution and angry discontent are transformed into a fierce aspiration echoing Tamburlaine:

> I am far better born than is the King,
> More like a king, more kingly in my thoughts.   (28-29)

This argument is more effective than his genealogical claim. That has moral contradictions which, although York does not see them, Shakespeare does. York says he is king by natural right, yet to prove Henry's impotence York admits himself a traitor whom his appointed sovereign cannot defeat. But legality counts for nothing when people settle arguments by force.

Buckingham demands to know why York comes to England armed in a time of peace. York temporizes: he came only to remove Somerset's influence over the King. But when Somerset suddenly appears, York defies the King:

> 'King' did I call thee? No, thou art not king;
> Not fit to govern and rule multitudes,
> Which darest not — no, nor canst not — rule a traitor.
> That head of thine doth not become a crown;
> Thy hand is made to grasp a palmer's staff,
> And not to grace an awful princely scepter.
> That gold must round engirt these brows of mine,
> Whose smile and frown, like to Achilles' spear,
> Is able with the change to kill and cure.
> Here is a hand to hold a scepter up,
> And with the same to act controlling laws.
> Give place: by heaven, thou shalt rule no more
> O'er him whom heaven created for thy ruler.   (93-105)

York wants his war. Margaret frustrates all Henry's hopes of peace by releasing Somerset. Salisbury says his conscience tells him York is "the rightful heir to England's royal seat" (line 178). War is inevitable. Henry receives the gruesome gift of Cade's head: "The head of Cade? Great God, how just art Thou!" (line 68). For him, God's spirit shows itself in the collapse of the rebels and the killing of Cade, not in the rebellion.

At the Battle of St. Albans, the King loses (V.ii-V.iii).

Civil war breaks out, the first battle of which concludes *2 Henry VI.* While York's forces grow irresistibly, Henry's lords leave him one by one. Eventually he must flee with Margaret, who urges haste:

> QUEEN: Away, my lord! You are slow. For shame, away!
> HENRY: Can we outrun the heavens?
>   Good Margaret, stay.
> QUEEN: What are you made of? You'll nor fight nor fly.
>   (V.ii.72-74)

The battle is lost, and he flees at the prompting of Young Clifford, bitter, pitiless, and a little berserk, who gives Shakespeare's most terrible pronouncement about war over his father's body:

> Henceforth I will not have to do with pity:
> Meet I an infant of the house of York,
> Into as many gobbets will I cut it
> As wild Medea young Absyrtus did;
> In cruelty will I seek out my fame.   (V.ii.56-60)

Henry keeps his "breastplate" of "a heart untainted," while the moral of the last part of the play is assimilated into a firm structure, a political and historical tragedy that serves later as the ground of *Julius Caesar.*

CONCLUSION

What primarily emerges from this early play is that the young Shakespeare is a theatrical master but still has to learn how to be a dramatic one. The poetry is not strong. It ranges from an inflated extreme,

> The gaudy, blabbing, and remorseful day
> Is crept into the bosom of the sea;
> And now loud howling wolves arouse the jades
> That drag the tragic melancholy night ...   (IV.i.1-4)

to the fine intensity of Young Clifford's battlefield imprecations (V.ii.31-65), Margaret's farewell to Suffolk, the wily and succinct logic of Warwick's apology for the Commons, and the warning to King Henry (III.ii.242-269). But the sure sense of theatre, dramatic design, and the first skills that draw great characters are hallmarks of Shakespeare's genius.

The development of Suffolk, first in his farewell with Margaret and then in his nobility with the pirates, is particularly notable. We see the young dramatist trying different techniques to develop character: with Cade's death scene in Iden's garden he uses the same method as with Suffolk; with York he uses a change in speech pattern from silent secrecy (in aside and soliloquy) to rhetorical bombast against Henry; with Humphrey he takes a well-known fifteenth century Christian humanist, one of the first in England, but creates no change of personality; and with Henry, one of the most difficult characters he ever tackled, all Shakespeare can do is make the character reactive, with the exception that he learns from Humphrey's death the way he wishes to live his life. With Margaret of Anjou, however, Shakespeare uses a medieval way of developing character: by showing her at different ages over four plays. In *1 Henry VI* she is introduced by being led captive onto the stage at the same time that the sexually promiscuous Joan is led off to be burned; Shakespeare intends us to see the parallel. Margaret's disruptive role becomes increasingly prominent as the story progresses and the *play world* sinks into chaos. A virago who defies and cuckolds her husband in *2 Henry VI*, she shows another face in her fear of losing Suffolk (which she does) and in the tenderness during their farewell. But this is merely another stage in her development, for she leads armies into battle and gloats at the murder of an innocent child in *3 Henry VI*, and becomes a raving prophetess in *Richard III*.

Henry VI Part 2 exemplifies the dramatic virtues of construction — forward action, continuity, tension, proportion, pace — which no playwright before Shakespeare had fully exploited. It is a playwright's play: the dramaturgy shows us how Shakespeare the playwright began. But it is also a director's and actor's play. Like the others in the trilogy, it has enormous theatrical energy if played in the continuous sequence of the Elizabethan manner. People pour across the stage in profusion. The play's rhythm pulses and carries the audience along with it. The major roles have made the careers of some actors. The lesser characters, too, reward the performers: the death scenes of the Cardinal and Cade, for example, are splendid sequences for players to develop. And many of the tiny roles are a delight to perform. If, in truth, *2 Henry VI* is Shakespeare's first play, it is a breathtaking achievement.

HENRY VI, PART 3

THE NIGHTMARE IN ACTION

The War of the Roses, begun in *2 Henry VI* when the lords chose the roses, white and red, is now a stark and horrifying reality. In *Part 3* we see a world of almost unrelieved cruelty. The nightmare of civil war affects everyone as the violent struggle of Lancaster and York rages across the stage. England swims in blood. Queen Margaret gloats over York before he is slaughtered, and impales his head on the gates of the town. Clifford kills York's young son, Rutland, and then Clifford himself is killed. And Henry VI and the Prince of Wales are both murdered by York's hunchbacked and venomous son Richard, eventually Richard III.

England, and those who live in it, is drowning in the vortex of a tempest. This major image of the play is treated in a variety of ways, one of which is Margaret's elaborate ship metaphor:

> We will not from the helm to sit and weep,
> But keep our course, though the rough wind say no,
> From shelves and rocks that threaten us with wrack.
> As good to chide the waves as speak them fair.
> And what is Edward but a ruthless sea?
> What Clarence but a quicksand of deceit?
> And Richard but a ragged fatal rock?
> All these the enemies to our poor bark.   (V.iv.21-28)

Those who act in violent and horrific ways become helpless ships struggling against the swell or swept onwards before the tumultuous wind. This storm, a chaos which human actions create, is an arbitrary force. Shakespeare creates his first commanding metaphor which, with maturity, becomes the storm of *King Lear* and *The Tempest*. In *3 Henry VI* everyone is dying of thirst, apart from gentle Henry: their ruthless lust for power is parching their throats. The sun, usually the symbol of majesty and fecundity, breeds flies, attracts gnats, and parches the entrails. In its deadly heat men burn and shrivel up.

STRUCTURE

The dilemma addressed by the trilogy has, in *3 Henry VI*, become, should a strong but Machiavellian nobility depose a weak but Christian king? Implicitly the answer is no, but the evils on both sides are vividly drawn. A Yorkist defeat is balanced by a Lancastrian defeat. Act V answers Act I as York answers Margaret. The murder of York's son is answered by the murder of Margaret's son — in fact, Shakespeare's design has a careful antithetical structure.

The structure is also remarkably simple and quite unlike that of any other Shakespearean play. It pulses onwards in changing rhythms, all but one of violent action. Alternating Interludes relieve the tension. There is no natural break, and, despite the act and scene divisions of later editors, we must assume the Lord Chamberlain's Men performed the play in one sequence of seven Movements:

[1] The initial confrontation begins a cyclic form which alternately increases and releases tension.

[2] The crisis of the Second Movement is York's murder.

[3] York's son becomes Edward IV, and Henry's capture follows.

[4] Edward's rescinding of his marriage ties to Bona Dea unites the French King, Queen Margaret, and Warwick. In the modern theatre, if there is an interval it is taken here.

[5] Clarence switches sides, Edward IV is captured, and Henry is temporarily restored.

[6] Edward recaptures Henry. Clarence changes sides again.

[7] Edward finally wins. Henry VI and his son are murdered.

Simple though the structure may be, the alternation of tensions in comparatively swift scenes keeps the audience on the edge of their seats.

ACTION

The First Movement: The Confrontation

Parliament House: after the Battle of St. Albans, York and his sons meet Henry and his lords. They agree that Henry will be king for life, with York as his heir. Margaret and the Prince of Wales attack Henry for disinheriting his son (I.i).

This impressive scene has many tensions to grip the audience. The focus is on two issues: legitimacy, where the arguments are futile and tragic; and the effects of the conflict on people and the realm. York and his sons enter the Parliament House, boasting of their bravery in the battle and scoffing at the "fearful king"

          whose cowardice

Hath made us by-words to our enemies.   (25, 41-42)

York seats himself on the throne. Henry enters, and he proves their description true as he urges patience on his followers. His supporter, Clifford, is exasperated:

Patience is for poltroons, such as he [York];

He durst not sit here had your father lived.   (62-63)

"Will you we show our title to the crown?" asks York. "If not, our swords shall plead it in the field" (lines 102-103). Henry bristles:

What title hast thou, traitor, to the crown?

Thy father was, as thou art, Duke of York;

Thy grandsire, Roger Mortimer, Earl of March.

I am the son of Henry the Fifth,

Who made the Dauphin and the French to stoop

And seized upon their towns and provinces.   (104-109)

Warwick replies sharply, "Talk not of France, sith thou hast lost it all" (line 110). Our sympathies towards Henry are divided. In one of his few forceful moments he says:

Thinkest thou that I will leave my kingly throne,

Wherein my grandsire and my father sat?

No; first shall war unpeople this my realm;

Ay, and their colours, often borne in France,

And now in England to our hearts' great sorrow,

Shall be my winding-sheet. Why faint you, lords?
My title's good, and better far than his. (124-130)
But Warwick challenges him: "Prove it Henry, and thou shalt be King" (line 131). Henry begins bravely but from a bad position:

KING: Henry the Fourth by conquest got the crown.
YORK: 'Twas by rebellion against his king.
KING: *(Aside)* I know not what to say; my title's weak.
Tell me, may not a king adopt an heir?
YORK: What then?
KING: And if he may, then am I lawful king;
For Richard, in the view of many lords,
Resigned the crown to Henry the Fourth,
Whose heir my father was, and I am his.
YORK: He rose against him, being his sovereign,
And made him to resign his crown perforce.
(132-142)

Ironically, York's argument is similar to Bolingbroke's. Exeter says:

he could not so resign his crown
But that the next heir should succeed and reign
(145-146)

and takes his stand for York: "My conscience tells me he is lawful king" (line 150). But Clifford dismisses all such technicalities:

King Henry, be thy title right or wrong,
Lord Clifford vows to fight in thy defence. (159-160)

Warwick copies his methods, stamps his foot, and his armed troops appear. In this realm, force conquers all. Henry has already realized this:

Ah, know you not the city favours them,
And they have troops of soldiers at their beck? (67-68)

They make a deal. Henry can reign for life if he disinherits his son in favour of York and his heirs, and if York swears to end the civil war. Henry agrees not because he is cowardly but to vainly right the old wrong done to Richard II. But abdication would also be wrong: Henry would break his own sworn oaths. Neither peace nor unity results.

The Prince of Wales protests,

Father, you cannot disinherit me;
If you be King, why should not I succeed? (226-227)

Henry explains he was forced. Queen Margaret exclaims, "Enforced thee! Art thou King, and wilt be forced?" (line 230). She calls him a coward:

> Had I been there, which am a silly woman,
> The soldiers should have tossed me on their pikes
> Before I would have granted to that act.   (243-245)

These events did not occur in history. According to Hall's *Chronicle*, a parliament attended by York (but not Henry, who was in prison) proclaimed Henry king, to be succeeded by York. Shakespeare makes the event into a personal confrontation between the two men in a scene of great tension.

Interlude

> *York and his sons hear that Margaret is nearby with a large army. The peace broken, they go off to war (I.ii).*

The Second Movement: The Battle of Wakefield

> *York's young son, Rutland, is killed by Clifford (I.iii).*

> *York is executed by Clifford and Margaret (I.iv).*

In this vicious and gruesome sequence the young Shakespeare suddenly creates the highly meaningful metaphor of the Player King, which becomes a key to many of his later plays. In *2 Henry VI* York said that he would

> stir up in England some black storm
Shall blow ten thousand souls to heaven or hell.

> (III.i.349-350)

When York is captured, Margaret says he

> raught at mountains with outstretchèd arms,
> Yet parted but the shadow with his hand.   (I.iv.68-69)

Suddenly York is revealed as a ritual actor. He stands on a mole-hill much like a Player King, the focus of rural festivities, whose achievements are illusory, not real. Margaret taunts him:

> What! Was it you that would be England's king?
> Was't you that revelled in our parliament
> And made a preachment of your high descent?   (70-72)

The Queen prolongs his life in order to degrade and mock him:

> Where are your mess of sons to back you now?

> The wanton Edward, and the lusty George?
> And where's that valiant crook-back prodigy,
> Dicky your boy, that with his grumbling voice
> Was wont to cheer his dad in mutinies?   (73-77)

Where, she asks, is Rutland? In answer to her own question, Margaret thrusts a handkerchief stained with the boy's blood into York's face.

> And if thine eyes can water for his death,
> I give thee this to dry thy cheeks withal.   (82-83)

As York's death scene unfolds, its playlike quality increases. Margaret says:

> And I, to make thee mad, do mock thee thus.
> Stamp, rave, and fret, that I may sing and dance.
> Thou wouldst be fee'd, I see, to make me sport;
> York cannot speak, unless he wear a crown.
> A crown for York! And, lords, bow low to him;
> Hold you his hands whilst I do set it on.
> *[She puts a paper crown upon his head.]*
> Ay, marry, sir, now looks he like a king!   (90-96)

The paper crown becomes Margaret's payment given in advance to York, the tragedian, for his performance. But he can respond in kind:

> She-wolf of France, but worse than wolves of France,
> Whose tongue more poisons than the adder's tooth!
>   (111-112)

He denounces Margaret as the antithesis of every feminine virtue:

> O tiger's heart wrapped in a woman's hide!
> How couldst thou drain the lifeblood of the child,
> To bid the father wipe his eyes withal,
> And yet be seen to bear a woman's face?
> Women are soft, mild, pitiful, and flexible;
> Thou stern, obdurate, flinty, rough, remorseless.
>   (137-142)

York's anguished speech, famous among the Elizabethan audience, was used by Shakespeare's detractor, Robert Greene. Holinshed has nothing like it. Shakespeare invents this whole sequence: he formalizes the violence so that the conflict is implacable. He turns York into a Player King who, accepting a role cruelly forced on him, makes it so poignant that even

Northumberland is moved to tears. This Player King is as regal as Henry VI is not. When he cries, "There, take the crown, and with the crown my curse" (line 164), he remakes the act into a symbol of his defeat; by giving to Margaret the paper crown as the symbol of England's crown, he raises the scene to a significance his torturers do not intend. His drama is over: his illusory reign ends as they kill him. Shakespeare's use of the Player King is unique to him and can be traced from *3 Henry VI* to *The Tempest*.

Interlude

Warwick has lost the Battle of St. Albans; Henry has been re-captured by Margaret. Clarence brings new troops (II.i).

The conflicting armies arrive at York, and they harangue each other (II.ii).

Henry is led to battle, literally a prisoner of Margaret and Clifford. When Margaret asks if Henry is pleased to see the head of the slain York above the town gates, he answers:

Ay, as the rocks cheer them that fear their wrack;
To see this sight, it irks my very soul.
Withhold revenge, dear God! 'Tis not my fault,
Nor wittingly have I infringed my vow.   (II.ii.5-8)

Clifford severely admonishes him for refusing to fight and not protecting the rights of his son. Clifford uses images from the animal world, which is also symbolized by York's head. Henry opposes the world of tooth and claw by virtue and morality. He would leave his son something better:

Full well hath Clifford played the orator,
Inferring arguments of mighty force.
But, Clifford, tell me, didst thou ever hear
That things ill got had ever bad success?
And happy always was it for that son
Whose father for his hoarding went to hell?
I'll leave my son my virtuous deeds behind;
And would my father had left me no more!   (43-50)

Henry, looking down on the bloodshed, believes Christianity has led humanity beyond the beast, to which the Machiavels would return.

The Third Movement: The Battle of Towton (York)

Warwick vows revenge for his brother (II.iii).

Richard and Clifford fight (II.iv).

Henry contemplates his role; the King's party flees (II.v).

Clifford dies. York's eldest son is to be King Edward IV (II.vi).

When Warwick hears his brother is killed, his momentary isolation from the battle seems to be like an audience at a play. He asks his companions:

> Why stand we like soft-hearted women here,
> Wailing our losses, whiles the foe doth rage;
> And look upon, as if the tragedy
> Were played in jest by counterfeiting actors?
>
> (II.iii.25-28)

Henry had refused to leave the battle when Margaret ordered it (II.ii), but now he withdraws (II.v), seats himself on a molehill (like York's molehill at Wakefield, a stage for acting the loss of a crown) and lets the battle rage. To cure his "grief and woe," he creates a substitute role: the ancient image of the virtuous shepherd tending his flock in an ordered, simple life, so needed in the king and kingdom:

> So many hours must I tend my flock,
> So many hours must I take my rest,
> So many hours must I contemplate,
> So many hours must I sport myself;
> So many days my ewes have been with young,
> So many weeks ere the poor fools will ean [bear young],
> So many years ere I shall shear the fleece.   (II.v.31-37)

Yet Henry cannot play this shepherd role as he defines it. He is both the spectator who observes and the presenter who interprets the tragedy. Here Henry resembles Richard II but without Richard's horror at his loss of identity. Henry has a vision of "a Son that hath kill'd his Father" followed by "a Father that hath kill'd his Son" — double emblems of England's spiritual disintegration. This vision was a high point in the Seale production, where, accompanied by drum and trumpet, it became a joint chorale with Henry gesticulating wildly as the lights went down.

Clifford, dying, judges the man he has supported with his life:

> And, Henry, hadst thou swayed as kings should do,
> Or as thy father and his father did,
> Giving no ground unto the house of York,
> They never then had sprung like summer flies;
> I and ten thousand in this luckless realm
> Had left no mourning widows for our death;
> And thou this day hadst kept thy chair in peace.
>
> (II.vi.14-20)

Interlude

Deposed by Edward IV, Henry hid in Scotland. Now he returns to England where he is captured by foresters (III.i).

This scene is often misinterpreted in the theatre and by critics. Far from being weak and abject, Henry shows his strong Christian beliefs despite his difficult circumstances. He thinks that, by losing his crown, he has lost the freedom to enjoy the land, the responsibility he has sworn to fulfill for God, and the ability to help his subjects.

> No, Harry, Harry, 'tis no land of thine;
> Thy place is filled, thy sceptre wrung from thee,
> Thy balm washed off wherewith thou wast anointed;
> No bending knee will call thee Caesar now,
> No humble suitors press to speak for right,
> No, not a man comes for redress of thee;
> For how can I help them and not myself?   (15-21)

Shakespeare connected identity and kingship in *Part 2* when York said:

> King did I call thee? No, thou art not king;
> Not fit to govern and rule multitudes. (*Part 2* V.i.93-94)

Now that Henry, the true king, is deposed he has neither an individuality nor a title. So, captured by the forest-keepers, he cannot tell them who he is:

> KING: More than I seem, and less than I was born to;
> A man at least, for less I should not be;
> And men may talk of kings, and why not I?

2 KEEP: Ay, but thou talkest as if thou wert a king.

KING: Why, so am I, in mind, and that's enough.

2 KEEP: But if thou be a king, where is thy crown?

KING: My crown is in my heart, not on my head;
Not decked with diamonds and Indian stones,
Nor to be seen; my crown is called content,
A crown it is that seldom kings enjoy. (56-65)

In the theatre Henry can be played as abject at this point, but his words show the proper humility required of a Christian king. Henry is patient, intelligent, and resourceful. He does not plead with his subjects. He instructs them by the questioning of the patient teacher, then by example:

KING: But did you never swear, and break an oath?

KEEP: No, never such an oath, nor will not now.

KING: Where did you dwell when I was King of England?

KEEP: Here in this country, where we now remain.

KING: I was anointed King at nine months old;
My father and my grandfather were kings,
And you were sworn true subject unto me;
And tell me, then, have you not broke your oaths?

KEEP: No, for we were subjects but while you were King.

KING: Why, am I dead? Do I not breathe a man?
Ah, simple men, you know not what you swear!
Look, as I blow this feather from my face,
And as the air blows it to me again,
Obeying with my wind when I do blow,
And yielding to another when it blows,
Commanded always by the greater gust;
Such is the lightness of you common men.
But do not break your oaths; for of that sin
My mild entreaty shall not make you guilty.
Go where you will, the King shall be commanded;
And be you kings, command, and I'll obey.
(72-93)

Henry commands here; in another time, he might have been a fine king.

The Fourth Movement: Marriage Arrangements

*The widowed Lady Grey wishes to possess her husband's
lands and appeals to Edward IV who agrees if she will be
his mistress. When she will not, he proposes marriage.
Henry is captured and taken to the Tower (III.ii).*

The Machiavels are in power, and their brutish desires lead
them to defy the moral law — in all Shakespeare's histories,
moral consciousness must be obeyed if people and society are
to survive. York had defied loyalty when his insanely selfish lust
for power threw the realm into chaos. Now Edward, his eldest
son, succumbs to sexual lust. Then Richard, obsessed by the
same ambition as his father, feels himself in hell

Until my misshaped trunk that bears this head
Be round impalèd with a glorious crown.   (170-171)

His soliloquy, one of Shakespeare's earliest pieces of imaginative self-disclosure, reveals Richard's frenzy to satisfy his tor-
menting desire:

And I — like one lost in a thorny wood,
That rents the thorns, and is rent with the thorns,
Seeking a way and straying from the way,
Not knowing how to find the open air,
But toiling desperately to find it out —
Torment myself to catch the English crown.   (174-179)

He resolves that

from that torment I will free myself,
Or hew my way out with a bloody axe.   (180-181)

*Margaret asks Lewis XI of France for help. Warwick
makes Edward's offer to marry Lewis' daughter. At news
of Edward's marriage, Lewis is angry. Warwick changes
sides. He and Margaret go to England with French help,
agreeing that the Prince of Wales will marry Warwick's
daughter (III.iii).*

When they hear Edward has already married, Warwick, dis-
honoured, asks,

Did I put Henry from his native right?
And am I guerdoned at the last with shame?   (190-191)

Lewis, using "play" to ironically express scorn, says to a messenger,

tell false Edward, thy supposèd king,
That Lewis of France is sending over masquers
To revel it with him and his new bride.   (223-225)

Interlude

Edward threatens to marry Clarence off (IV.i).

*Clarence changes sides and marries Warwick's second
daughter (IV.ii).*

The Fifth Movement: Edward's Capture

*Warwick captures Edward (taken to the Archbishop of
York) and goes to free Henry from the Tower (IV.iii).*

Interlude

Queen Elizabeth (Grey) flees to sanctuary (IV.iv).

Edward IV escapes (IV.v).

*Henry is restored, but news of Edward's escape leads
young Richmond to be sent to Brittany for safety (IV.vi).*
Henry lays his hand hopefully on the head of young
Richmond, who will one day rise out of the ruins as Henry VII:

If secret powers
Suggest but truth to my divining thoughts,
This pretty lad will prove our country's bliss.
His looks are full of peaceful majesty,
His head by nature framed to wear a crown,
His hand to wield a sceptre, and himself
Likely in time to bless a regal throne.   (IV.vi.68-74)

The Sixth Movement: Edward's Return

*Edward and Richard take the town of York. Edward is
"persuaded" to proclaim himself king again (IV.vii).*

Edward takes London and re-captures Henry (IV.viii).

Henry is not a saint: he resents the usurpation of his throne, and in his joy at Warwick's defection to his side he flatteringly refers to that Machiavel as "my Hector and my Troy's true hope" (IV.viii.25), which is a weak act by his own Christian standards. He thinks he should be loved by his people:

> My pity hath been balm to heal their wounds,
> My mildness hath allayed their swelling griefs,
> My mercy dried their water-flowing tears.   (41-43)

But he is out of touch with political reality. His lords do not contest this claim, they simply think it makes him incapable.

Interlude

Warwick parleys with Edward at Coventry. Clarence changes sides again and returns to his brothers (V.i).

The Seventh Movement: The Battles of Barnet and Tewkesbury

Warwick dies as Margaret's forces arrive (V.ii).

Edward reorganizes for Tewkesbury (V.iii).

There he and Margaret parley (V.iv).

Edward captures her and the Prince of Wales. Edward, Clarence and Richard kill her son. Richard goes "To make a bloody supper in the Tower" (V.v).

Finale

Richard kills Henry (V.vi).

Edward banishes Margaret to France while Richard plots against his brothers (V.vii).

As Henry is murdered by Richard, he is strong and heroic. He is occupied with the death of his son:

> I, Daedalus; my poor boy, Icarus;
> Thy father, Minos, that denied our course;
> The sun that seared the wings of my sweet boy,

Thy brother Edward, and thyself, the sea
Whose envious gulf did swallow up his life.   (V.vi.21-25)
Icarus is the Prince of Wales, Minos is York, the searing sun is
Edward IV, the drowning sea is Richard, and Henry is
Daedalus, who by tradition is crippled and awkward. Henry is a
crippled ruler in a wicked world. He then envisions Richard's
ascendancy:

And thus I prophesy, that many a thousand
Which now mistrust no parcel of my fear,
And many an old man's sigh, and many a widow's,
And many an orphan's water-standing eye —
Men for their sons,' wives for their husbands,'
Orphans for their parents' timeless death —
Shall rue the hour that ever thou wast born.   (37-43)

Richard stabs him in mid-sentence, and Henry dies asking
God's forgiveness for his own sins. His dying words to Richard,
"O God forgive my sins, and pardon thee" (line 60), are pious,
gentle, and strong. The new peace of England is symbolized by
King Edward's promise of time given to "stately triumphs,
mirthful comic shows" (V.vii.43).

THE SUCCESS OF THE TRILOGY

Like all of Shakespeare's plays, the *Henry VI* trilogy operates on
many levels. These plays present, in dialogue and action, the
legal and political problems of legitimacy and power in the
Wars of the Roses. There is no final answer. To Shakespeare,
undisputed legal succession is the strongest moral argument to
support royal power. Yet the *right* to govern cannot be separated from the *ability* to govern.

Henry VI, a weak man but a peaceful Christian, lacks the
ability to wield power, command authority, or inspire confidence. He cannot control the Machiavels who surround him.
This inability breeds their ambitions and invites their contempt. But by the end Henry has grown: his faith is strong, and
in the theatre he arouses our sympathy. He differs from all of
Shakespeare's other kings in that he has no "mask": his public
and private personalities are the same. No other king intends
so much good for his kingdom or feels his subjects' sufferings
so keenly.

Henry sets the actor a monumental task: to create the "good" in the theatre is a far more difficult problem than the acting of evil. His actions and responses show that he alone believes in the natural dignity of humanity. He is not "bad," because he cannot govern by force or deceit; that is the view of the Machiavels. Henry might be a good king — if the wicked would let him.

It is theatrically right for Richard to kill Henry: evil overcomes good; the ultimately wicked strikes down the pious King, destroying the gentle Christian who stands as a rebuke to his brutal viciousness. The murder has a strongly symbolic quality. It brings together on the stage, alone, the personifications of Lancaster and York, who embody the conflict between kindliness and ferocity that underlies the action of *Henry VI*.

Richard is a gift to an actor. It is he who makes the greatest impact on the stage. "He's sudden if a thing comes in his head," says Edward (V.v.86), as his deformed brother is on his way to the Tower "to make a bloody supper" of King Henry. The most evil of the stage-Machiavels, he can suppress his humanity.

> MARG: His sons, he says, shall give their words for him.
> YORK: Will you not, sons?
> EDW: Aye, noble father, if our words will serve.
> RICH: And if words will not, then our weapons shall.
> (*Part 2* V.i.137-140)

His is a stunning portrait: his macabre promise that young Clifford "shall sup with Jesu Christ to-night" (*Part 2* V.i.214); the melodramatic flourish as he throws down Somerset's head and says, "Speak thou for me, and tell them what I did" (I.i.16); his vulgarity in his asides to Clarence during Edward's courtship of Lady Grey (III.ii.111-117); and the irony in his assurances to Edward that he does not disapprove of the match:

> No, God forbid that I should wish them severed
> Whom God hath joined together; ay, and 'twere pity
> To sunder them that yoke so well together. (IV.i.21-23)

The ultimate villain, he wishes his brothers thoroughly "wasted, marrow, bones, and all" (III.ii.125) to clear his own path to the throne. His evil is revealed to the audience in two major soliloquies. First, Richard confides that his deformity keeps him from finding "heaven in a lady's lap" (III.ii.148). His pleasures must lie elsewhere:

> I'll make my heaven to dream upon the crown
> And, whiles I live, t' account this world but hell,
> Until my misshaped trunk that bears this head
> Be round impalèd with a glorious crown. (III.ii.168-171)

"Why, I can smile, and murder whiles I smile," the arch-hypocrite proudly announces (III.ii.182):

> I can add colours to the chameleon,
> Change shapes with Proteus for advantages,
> And set the murderous Machiavel to school.
> Can I do this, and cannot get a crown?
> Tut, were it farther off, I'll pluck it down. (III.ii.191-195)

In the second soliloquy, delivered after he has stabbed Henry, Richard declares that his soul will be as deformed as his body:

> The midwife wondered and the women cried
> 'O, Jesus bless us, he is born with teeth!'
> And so I was, which plainly signified
> That I should snarl and bite and play the dog.
> Then, since the heavens have shaped my body so,
> Let hell make crooked my mind to answer it.
> I have no brother, I am like no brother;
> And this word 'love,' which greybeards call divine,
> Be resident in men like one another
> And not in me; I am myself alone.   (V.vi.74-83)

Richard of Gloucester is Shakespeare's first great character, and his portrayal in *Richard III* is brilliantly anticipated in *3 Henry VI*. Robert Atkins (Old Vic, 1923) was renowned for the growth of Richard in the two plays.* Richard becomes another kind of Player King. Most of Shakespeare's Player Kings from York to Prospero are creatures of the Renaissance rather than of the Middle Ages, and are created by Shakespeare with a wealth of meanings largely unexplored before his time. In this trilogy, Richard of York is not only the first of Shakespeare's Player Kings, but the one who reminds us of the most ancient traditions; in its memory of a ritual past, the performance is very disturbing. But Richard of Gloucester is fully conscious

---

* See Sprague (1964).

that he is playing the king. In *Richard III* he does so with vicious glee, and this self-consciousness is even more frightening.

The trilogy does not propose hard political solutions. They are only vaguely plays of ideas. Shakespeare's intense anger lies behind them, but, except that the shameful underside of political life is shown, it is aimed at human actions in general. Since the 1950s, more people have seen the *Henry VI* plays than in all the previous centuries of their existence. They have been seen on television and widely on stage in Britain, Canada, and the United States. Why this sudden popularity? Simply stated, the plays result in great theatre, and they are good if not great literature.

Literary critics do not like melodrama, and are always astonished that *Richard III* is Shakespeare's most popular play after *Hamlet*. But all four plays of the War of the Roses are melodramatic, and it is not surprising that Shakespeare's action-packed plays have the power to thrill, particularly among young audiences. By compacting history and embodying opposing forces in individuals, Shakespeare increases our excitement. His brilliant construction, different in each of the three plays, sweeps us along, and, out of the ruins of a society, emerges the monstrous figure of Richard of Gloucester, ready to play in a script of his own.

RICHARD III

THE PLAY OF PARADOXES

The Tragedy of Richard III is a remarkable play for many reasons. It tells the story of one of the world's greatest villains, the ultimate horror figure with a crooked mind and a crooked body. He commits the most evil deeds but never repents; rather, he revels in his crimes against humanity, and, when he is killed at the end, he still enjoys them.

Paradoxically, however, *Richard III* was an enormous success when Shakespeare wrote it, and it remains one of the most popular plays today. Not that we should confuse Shakespeare's Richard with the actual king: the historical Richard was not so wicked as he is painted; it is still an unsolved question whether he committed any of the murders charged against him by his enemies. In Shakespeare's play, however, he commits virtually all possible sins with lip-smacking relish. As he does so, we in the audience enjoy ourselves thoroughly.

What are we to make of this paradox? In the first place, we overcome evil less by repudiating it than by identifying with it. This is the case in Aeschylus' conclusion to the *Oresteia:* as G. Wilson Knight points out, the Furies or Eumenides, which are both the evil and avenging powers, are only placated by being accepted and even honoured as part of the community; their home is to be *below* the city — as though there are forces in all of us which must be both recognized and hidden from sight.*

How can we sympathize with such evils as the Furies or Richard? The answer, according to Aeschylus, Shakespeare, and most great dramatists, is: by looking inwards — by admitting our own worst thoughts, both conscious and unconscious. Then we discover that the evil figures on the stage are ourselves

---

* Knight (1964) 310-321.

magnified. But if they are bigger, they are not necessarily worse; and if our own evil actions seem small compared with Richard's, they are still evils. Good and evil are two sides of the same coin. While we identify with Richard, we can repudiate his evil acts without necessarily repudiating his soul. Embedded in his acts are some values which await their release through us.

By creating such a fascinating figure who performs such terrible evils, Shakespeare allows us, the audience, to do part of the work. We contribute our perspective on these evil events and on this evil man. We provide the other side of the coin, and the "truth" emerges from this relation. The performance of the play, therefore, becomes a "moral" experience to us. But *Richard III* is a great advance on the Moralities of late Medieval and early Tudor times, whether Catholic or Protestant. They posed the moral questions and gave, supposedly, the only possible answers. Shakespeare, in the greatest of the humanist traditions, does not give us the answers. We, in the audience, juxtapose our own side of the coin — our own "good" — and contrast it with Richard's evil. What happens to us in the playhouse is that, by identifying with Richard, we allow our own values to emerge. Values are not forced upon us. Shakespeare gives us the opportunity to make up our own minds — a fundamental human freedom.

In the second place we overcome this paradox of enjoying the evil in *Richard III* by relating it to our experience in life. When Shakespeare wrote this play, about 1592 or 1593, the Elizabethan audience was eager for plays about English history. He was still a young man, but this was his fourth play on the subject: he had already written the three parts of *Henry VI*, which ended at the point where *Richard III* begins, and he was probably about to revise *King John* in the version we now have. The audiences thought such plays were like mirrors in which they could see what had happened to England in past crises and, importantly, what might happen to the realm after the death of Queen Elizabeth. Shakespeare's view of the problem of England's future was that the country should unite behind the present monarch, and he emphasizes the dangers of division and civil war. When Shakespeare depicts these, as in all his early English histories, we see the horrors that can befall the country.

While the theme of political chaos had a direct appeal to the Elizabethans, it has an equal if not greater attraction in our own time. The twentieth century world is at least as divided as that of late Elizabethan times. It has given human beings the most appalling experiences of bloodshed and inhumanity: two world wars and their notorious concentration camps, "the killing fields" of Southeast Asia, interracial and political massacres of millions and in all parts of the world, and the emergence of monstrous individuals whose names are synonymous with horrifying evil — Hitler, Pol Pot, Stalin, Idi Amin, and many others. Our experience of *Richard III*, performed in a playhouse, has direct meaning for us all.

Another reason we enjoy the evil in *Richard III* is that it is so dramatic, a play for the stage. Shakespeare does not pretend that it is lifelike. We in the playhouse recognize that we are witnessing a theatrical fiction performed by an actor "as if" he is Richard of Gloucester. It is, first and foremost, a work of theatrical art: Shakespeare has so ritualized the action that it is "bigger" than life, more significant than ordinary experience.

We overcome evil by identifying with it, and by relating our theatre experience to our life, and then making up our own minds about our values. Thus its appeal to us is immediate.

Richard III was Shakespeare's first great smash hit, a sudden leap up from his three plays on the reign of King Henry VI. The English court and all of London talked about it, and Richard Burbage made his reputation by creating the role of Richard III. It has remained a favourite role for virtuoso actors ever since. *Richard III* is still a paradox, but it is one with important meanings for us all.

HISTORY OF THE PLAY

In the person of Richard of Gloucester, a Yorkist, Shakespeare had a historical subject worthy of his rapidly-maturing powers. His *Richard III* has a long and triumphant history in the theatre. Probably first performed in 1592-1593, it appears in several printed versions. The best is in the *First Folio*, but the earlier *First Quarto* (1597), and the five additional printings before the 1623 *Folio*, may in a few places give a better reading than the *First Folio*.

Shakespeare's ideas for the play had two origins: Richard in the perspective of the Tudor myth, and Seneca's tragedies about tyrants.

His major sources were the Elizabethan historians, mainly Holinshed's *Chronicles* (1587), much of which was taken from Edward Hall. Their Tudor myth [see *End Notes*] gave legitimacy to the Tudor monarchs: the deposing and killing of "the Lord's Anointed" (Richard II), the rightful king, by the House of Lancaster led by Bolingbroke, later Henry IV. This brought fundamental anarchy and, logically, led to the vicious barbarity of the Wars of the Roses. When, in *Richard III*, Elizabeth says, "All-seeing heaven, what a world is this!" she is describing the chaos of England: a world of absolute moral ill which everyone inherits — at least, until the arrival of the Earl of Richmond who, as Henry VII, becomes the first Tudor and the new "Lord's Anointed." Before that, everyone is tainted with the savagery and treachery of civil strife, and internally cursed with moral decay, so that there are only three kinds of people: the strong in evil, like Richard; the feebly wicked, like Clarence; and the helplessly guilt-tainted, like the lamenting women in their penitential psalm —

> All may be well; but, if God sort it so,
> 'Tis more than we deserve or I expect.   (II.iii.36-37)

For the Tudor historians, Richard was a murderer and a tyrant. As a result, *Richard III* has sometimes been disparaged as crude melodrama; but this is to misunderstand both the nature of the play and how it is written.

Shakespeare based his play on Sir Thomas More's *History of King Richard the Third* (c. 1513), where Richard is depicted as a monster, giving Shakespeare an ideal character for dramatization. More's misshapen Richard is both sinister and intriguing. Shakespeare's development of the portrait is dazzling. While More's Richard is clever, with sardonic humour and theatricality, he writes about him from a distance; like a Victorian missionary-explorer describing a native tribe which has (for him or her) revolting habits, More continually comments with moral outrage and disgust. But Shakespeare's Richard is exuberant and vital: he is heroic and wittily engaging, while his villainy is bluntly honest — he tells us all his secret plans in soliloquies and asides. Shakespeare does not humanize More's villain by giving him a guilty conscience, as in *The True Tragedy of Richard III* (1594), which Shakespeare quotes in *Hamlet*. But Shakespeare does make Richard's villainy believable and enjoyable: Richard becomes a wickedly cheeky comedian with a sardonic turn of mind. He is so enthusiastic in his villainy that others in the play seem grey and dreary by comparison.

The play *Richard III* was also influenced by the Latin tradition of Seneca, whose plays were the main model for classical tragedy in the sixteenth century. The Elizabethans thought that these Roman plays were full of political wisdom, and that some contained Machiavellian ideas — then being discussed by Shakespeare's contemporaries. Seneca's tyrants had fierce and unnatural passions, a lust for power, and a political philosophy that made fear, power, and will more important than love, legitimacy, and law. *Richard III* has more Senecan characteristics than any of the other history plays, and its hero is very like Seneca's tyrants. The earliest English play on Richard's life is the Latin *Richardus Tertius* of Thomas Legge, acted at Cambridge in 1580. This is very Senecan, with a Richard who is both a tyrant and a monster. It is unlikely that Shakespeare knew it, but he did know *The True Tragedy of Richard III* which, although not typically Senecan, has a Richard who is a tyrant and is called so. The idea of a tyrant, inherent in Elizabethan Richards, is also present in the narrative of Richard's ghost in *A Mirror for Magistrates*, a non-dramatic work which Shakespeare also knew.

Richard Burbage, a colleague of Shakespeare and the leading actor in his plays, was famous for playing the roles of Hamlet, Othello, and Lear — but was particularly identified with Richard III. John Manningham, a law student at the Middle Temple, wrote in his diary a story that once, when Burbage played Richard, a woman was so attracted by him that she invited him to come to her that night by the name of Richard III; Shakespeare, overhearing, sent his friend the message that "William the Conqueror came before Richard the Third."

In the Elizabethan theatre, most of *Richard III* takes place on the open-air platform stage, which the audience imagines as a street, a room in the palace, Bosworth Field, etc. The upper stage is used when Richard speaks to the Mayor and citizens. A curtain at the back of the main stage probably opened to disclose a throne in IV.ii, the only essential fixed property in the play. Before Bosworth, the tents of Richard and Richmond are pitched at the opposite sides of the stage, with their fronts open so that the audience can see them both; when they exit, the soldiers carry off the tents to clear the field for battle.

The initial success of *Richard III* has been repeated for succeeding generations of actors and audiences. Like *Hamlet*, it has never failed to hold the stage because it is an "actor's play." Essentially theatrical, it is inspired by the stage and by the actor's awareness of the power which a virtuoso performer has over his audiences.

The first major revival of the play was Colley Cibber's adaptation in 1700 that held the stage into the nineteenth century. Cibber cut the original text heavily and rewrote much; indeed, some of Cibber's own lines have become almost inseparable from the play, including "Off with his head, so much for Buckingham," and "Richard's himself again." David Garrick, the greatest actor of his time, used Cibber's text in a famous Richard (1741-1776) which, uniquely, he developed in each act of the play. George Frederick Cooke's diabolical Richard was admired (though not by Charles Lamb), both at Covent Garden and in New York, where Cooke died in 1812. Edmund Kean, one of the greatest English actors, took London by storm in 1814 as Shylock and as Richard III, in a production which Coleridge said was like "reading Shakespeare by flashes of lightning."* When Macready restored much of Shakespeare's original text in 1821 the public disapproved. It was not until Samuel Phelps at Sadler's Wells (1845) that a post-Shakespearean audience heard only Shakespeare's words. Charles Kean, son of Edmund, staged spectacular productions in New York in 1846 and in London in 1854. Later great Richards in England include Henry Irving, Robert Atkins, Balliol Holloway, Donald Wolfit, Laurence Olivier, Ian Holm, and Alan Howard.

Richard III was the first Shakespeare play acted professionally in the United States (1750); it was loved by Lincoln, who knew the monologue "Now is the winter of our discontent" by

---

* For stage history, see Eccles (1965), Sprague (1944, 1953, 1964), and Sprague and Trewin (1970).

heart. The first black theatre troupe in America, the African Company, opened in New York with *Richard III* acted by James Hewlett (1821). Also in that company was Ira Aldridge, the most famous black actor, who went abroad and played Richard and other roles all over Europe. Junius Brutus Booth, who made himself up to look like Kean, acted Richard at Covent Garden and then for many years coast-to-coast in America. Later great Richards in America include Edwin Booth, Edwin Forrest, John McCullough, Walter Hampden, John Barrymore, Hume Cronyn, and Kevin Kline.

The Stratford (Ontario) Shakespeare Festival opened in 1953 with Alec Guinness as Richard in a famous production by Tyrone Guthrie. Other fine Richards followed, including Christopher Plummer (1961), Alan Bates (1967), and Brian Bedford (1977).

In early silent films Richard was usually played by a stock actor, but Max Reinhardt directed a German film in 1919, with Conrad Veidt as Richard. Olivier in 1955 directed his great film of the play in colour and sound. Three television productions have been made in Britain: directed by Peter Dews in the series "An Age of Kings" (1960); acted by Ian Holm in the Royal Shakespeare Company's "The War of the Roses" (1964); and another directed by Jane Howell (1982).

The time gap between the Battle of Bosworth and the first performance of *Richard III* was approximately the same as between the Crimean War and our own time. My great-grandfather could have been in the Crimean War, and we all know of Florence Nightingale and the Charge of the Light Brigade. Similarly, the events in *Richard III* still reverberated in the audience at the first performance. They had a tradition of oral culture, and the names of Richard Crookback, the princes in the Tower, and Bosworth Field, were passed down by the audience's great-grandfathers to their families by word of mouth.

We can all relate to the poetic meanings in the play. The deformed Richard reflects the deformed life of England: Richard always swears by St. Paul who, according to one tradition, was deformed. The crown indicates, on the one hand, the secular power at which Richard and Richmond aim, and, on the other, the realm and the people. For Shakespeare the unconscious and the nightmares make the guilty fear that they will drown in the darkness of the deep and be accursed by the victims they have murdered. Paradox, in addition, is horrifying: everything has opposite meanings to what we expect. Not the least of these uncertainties is other people. In the play-world of Richard, whose emblem is the boar, how can we really know the people we meet?

THE ACTION

The dramatic action focuses on the criminal acts committed by a tyrant; these acts are punished by divine justice. As the play begins, Richard is a potential tyrant: he plots to murder those in his own Yorkist branch of the Plantagenet family who stand between him and the crown. He grows into a classic tyrant by the way he achieves the crown, and by the use of power for his own ends and not for the welfare of the realm. The audience follows this quite easily, as the plot is not complex. The identification of characters can be difficult, however, and the director must take care that the complex family relationships are made clear — "pointed," in theatrical terms.

The action of the play has a linear structure that reaches its major climax with the coronation of Richard (IV.ii). This is the central scene: until then Richard is winning, but thereafter he continually loses. The centrality of this scene, together with the lesser climaxes and tensions of the play, shows that the dramatic sequence has five Movements: Movement 1, Act I; Movement 2, Acts II.-III.iv; Movement 3, Acts III.v-IV.iii; Movement 4, Acts IV.iv-V.i; Movement 5, Act V.ii-V.iv.

Preliminary: *Henry VI Part 3*

The vendetta of Lancaster and York, two branches of the royal Plantagenets, led to cruel murders. Queen Margaret, wife of Henry VI, beheaded York whose sons (Edward, Richard, and George of Clarence) killed Henry and their son. York's eldest son became Edward IV with his queen, Elizabeth.

Shakespeare had shown Richard of Gloucester's will to achieve power in *3 Henry VI* and his plan to win the crown:

Why, I can smile, and murder whiles I smile,
And cry 'Content!' to that which grieves my heart,
And wet my cheeks with artificial tears,
And frame my face to all occasions...
I can add colors to the chameleon,
Change shapes with Proteus for advantages,
And set the murderous Machiavel to school.
Can I do this, and cannot get a crown?   (III.ii.182-194)

After killing Henry VI, Richard intended his brother, Clarence, to be next:

I have no brother, I am like no brother;
And this word 'love,' which graybeards call divine,
Be resident in men like one another
And not in me: I am myself alone.   (V.vi.80-83)

By the end of *Richard III*, Richard does indeed find he is himself alone.

The First Movement

Richard tells us he plots villainy. He arranges for Clarence to be taken to the Tower (I.i).

Now is the winter of our discontent
Made glorious summer by this sun of York ...   (1-2)

So Richard of Gloucester begins his famous soliloquy at the beginning of *Richard III* — one of Shakespeare's highest achievements and a major scene for a great actor. As Richard hobbles out on stage, he adapts the role of the medieval Vice and addresses the audience. Winter is now summer as Lancaster has given way to York, and the killing is over. It is time to live and love, but not for Richard. He ridicules the peaceful social order now that his elder brother has come to the throne as Edward IV. But —

He capers nimbly in a lady's chamber
To the lascivious pleasing of a lute.   (12-13)

Richard, however, is different:

But I, that am not shap'd for sportive tricks
Nor made to court an amorous looking-glass;
I, that am rudely stamped, and want love's majesty
To strut before a wanton ambling nymph;
I, that am curtailed of this fair proportion,

> Cheated of feature by dissembling Nature,
> Deformed, unfinished, sent before my time
> Into this breathing world, scarce half made up,
> And that so lamely and unfashionable
> That dogs bark at me as I halt by them —
> Why, I, in this weak piping time of peace,
> Have no delight to pass away the time,
> Unless to spy my shadow in the sun
> And descant on mine own deformity.
> And therefore, since I cannot prove a lover
> To entertain these fair well-spoken days,
> I am determined to prove a villain
> And hate the idle pleasures of these days.   (14-31)

He wants to create a new environment and begins by manipu-
lating the present: before tackling the king, he will first get rid
of his other brother, George, Duke of Clarence,

> To set my brother Clarence and the King
> In deadly hate the one against the other.   (34-35)

While this soliloquy resembles Richard's first soliloquy in *3
Henry VI*, there are important differences. His verbal style is ele-
gant, even studied. He savours and even "tastes" the alliterations,
antitheses, and rhetorical flourishes which are mere conventions. But Richard has no passion for the grandiose: he has left
behind his Marlovian hyperboles in the earlier play. Now his
speech is measured, and he wields words like a sword. Laurence
Olivier, in his film version of *Richard III*, captures Richard's vocal
fastidiousness as he phrases his lines with nicety and precision.

Richard's deformity represents a deformed world. As he
limps around the stage in his soliloquy, his curious body no
longer just prevents him from being "a man to be beloved" *(3
Henry VI*, III.ii.163); his twisted leg and shoulder have become
"like to a chaos" (I.i.161). He is not only misshapen, nor simply
a monster, but the epitome of disorder. Nor is he just the symbol
of chaos, or representing chaos: for the first three Movements,
at least, Richard is chaos; only later does he become a scapegoat.

Who is the real Richard? There are four simultaneous levels
of Richard as a person: he is the *dramatist* of his own "play within a play," who is brutally honest with us, the audience; he is a
consummate *actor* who knows exactly what he is doing; he wears
social masks with other persons in the play; and he is the "inner"
Richard — his *personality*.

Richard is a great player. But he does not explicitly refer to his ability in, or his plans for, play *acting*, as he does later in the play. In the soliloquy he *is* a player. However, the explicit theatrical imagery of the soliloquy establishes him as the dramatist of his own play, which is to be performed before us. This enables him to manipulate others — "Plots have I laid, inductions dangerous ..." (line 32). He is both a prologue and a puppet master; as he introduces the action he contrives and dominates. From the opening moments, Shakespeare has established the play as a theatrical event: Richard is telling us that *this performance* is "a play within a play" for which he is responsible. But it does not remain so. After the coronation and the murder of the princes in the Tower, Richard loses control of his creation; he alters from a dramatist to "one who is being played."

While he *is* a player in the soliloquy, he tells us, the audience, of the stratagems he dare not reveal to anyone else. We enjoy his confidences because his evil ambition is so dispassionate. He displays little personal malice or envy to us (at least, not obviously), and we identify with his sardonic humour and the sudden twists of his mind.

The most significant, and quite shocking, difference between this soliloquy and what Richard says in *3 Henry VI* lies in what he does *not* say here. In *3 Henry VI* Richard wanted the crown. But here he never specifically mentions to us a desire for it, although we infer it. Richard, the player, is amusing and reasonable: he does not seem tormented by his deformity, or driven to seek power by his own inferiority, or suffer from gnawing anguish, as he frankly tells us what he intends to do. Because he *is* a player, he is not embittered. Rather, he sounds bored: he wants work, something to do now the war is over, a goal worthy of his energy and talents. In the audience (*we* know that *he* knows differently) we are amused by his playing.

Even in this soliloquy, we cannot predict his calculated changes of mood. His melodramatic gestures strike us like lightning, and his incisive words and phrases affect others like rapiers. But he is not impulsive as a player: he has masterly control over his performance. Indeed, his reasonableness is much more frightening than his sudden outbursts of passion, which are as calculated as his acts of seeming piety. Yet, in his own twisted way, Richard is ascetic: he despises men who, like both Edward and Hastings, waste their time with lechery.

Shakespeare contracts historical time. We understand that *Richard III* begins shortly after the death of Henry VI (Lancaster) and the accession of Edward IV (York); this time period is confirmed as Anne accompanies the body of Henry VI towards burial (I.ii); almost immediately comes the illness of Edward IV (I.iii) and his death (II.ii). Yet in history Henry VI was killed in 1471 and Edward died in 1483. These changes to history are for dramatic purposes: his Richard aims to eliminate the principal heirs so that on Edward's death he will remain the sole Yorkist survivor with an immediate claim to the throne. Shakespeare invented most of the history in the first act. In actuality, Richard murdered Henry VI in 1471; in 1478 Edward IV (not Richard) had Clarence condemned to death, drowned in wine at the Tower; and at the period of the play, Queen Margaret was living in France.

The first three acts consist almost entirely of playlets staged by Richard, with the exception of Clarence's death and the lamentations by Richard's female victims. As his soliloquy ends, Richard plays for Clarence's benefit the role of devoted brother. Clarence is going to the Tower under Edward IV's orders, not knowing that this results from Richard's plot. Richard is in high spirits as he sardonically says to Clarence: "Your imprisonment shall not be long" (line 114). With his sharp intelligence, Richard catches his victims off guard. Clarence is led off, convinced that Richard will save him. He has just exited when Richard muses ironically:

> Simple plain Clarence! I do love thee so
> That I will shortly send thy soul to heaven ...

Then, imitating Clarence:

> If heaven will take the present at our hands.   (118-120)

Once he is rid of his brothers, he thinks, the world will be free for him "to bustle in" (line 152).

Richard successfully woos the Lady Anne (I.ii).

In a scene entirely invented by Shakespeare, Richard woos the Lady Anne "for a secret close intent" (I.i.158) — to link the two branches of the Plantagenets. She is the daughter of the late Earl of Warwick and also the wife (really the betrothed) to

Prince Edward, whom, with his father Henry VI, Richard has killed. It is Henry's coffin that Lady Anne stands over, as Richard approaches her and, rising to the challenge, overwhelms her with a mixture of impudence and flattery. The scene, which is not even crucial for the plot, demonstrates Richard's almost diabolical power. In a *tour de force* as a player, Richard leads Anne from her initial horror towards fascination. It is more of a rape than a courtship: on the surface he seems cringing and slimy, but he bullies her, then mocks her high moral tone by appeals to Christian charity. She curses him and any woman he marries. He does not try to persuade her of his sincerity, but takes the ludicrous role of a sighing Petrarchan lover and confesses that he has murdered her husband and father-in-law to win her! She cannot believe the ridiculous lie that he did so because of her beauty, but she prefers his flattery to admitting his brutal contempt for her. She finally stops cursing him and appears willing to become his wife. His triumph complete, Richard has every right to crow:

> Was ever woman in this humour wooed?
> Was ever woman in this humour won?
> I'll have her, but I will not keep her long.
> What? I that killed her husband and his father
> To take her in her heart's extremest hate,
> With curses in her mouth, tears in her eyes,
> The bleeding witness of my hatred by,
> Having God, her conscience, and these bars against me,
> And I no friends to back my suit at all
> But the plain devil and dissembling looks?
> And yet to win her! All the world to nothing!
>
> (I.ii.227-237)

He stresses his histrionic skill whereby he has even managed, he suggests sarcastically, to make her believe in his physical beauty:

> I do mistake my person all this while!
> Upon my life, she finds, although I cannot,
> Myself to be a marvellous proper man.   (252-254)

This scene, together with the parallel scene with Elizabeth (IV.iv), gave problems to the critics from Garrick's time. Primarily, they doubted that a man would woo, and a woman respond, in such ways. Needless to say, what the scene lacks in the reading it does not lack on the stage, and it has always been popular with audiences.

Hall reported that Henry VI's body lay in state at St. Paul's and then was conveyed to the Monastery at Chertsey at night, with few in attendance. This would have suited Elizabethan staging but not that of the nineteenth century. John Barrymore shocked audiences by cutting down the funeral retinue of "from 70 to 80 people" (before whom Richard's wooing would, indeed, have been ludicrous) to a small group at the rear of the stage.

Richard counterfeits among his enemies, and he receives Margaret's curse (I.iii).

Edward IV is very ill. His wife, Queen Elizabeth, and her relations, the Lords Rivers and Grey, are worried that, if Edward dies, the young Prince of Wales will be put into the trust of Richard. The days of the Lancaster-York vendetta are long over, and even the memories of atrocities are almost forgotten (except by Margaret). Most people in *Richard III* want to forget the past and how they became eminent. They are opportunists playing their respectable roles in society. Here Richard takes the role of an easy victim, incapable of dissembling, and loathing such behaviour in others, who repents any crimes he may have inadvertently committed. But Queen Elizabeth recalls enough of the past to be rightly worried about her children, while old Queen Margaret carries her bloody memories with her. "My hair doth stand on end to hear her curses," Hastings remarks (line 303). But she saves her greatest curse for the worst of them all, the "poisonous bunch-back'd toad" (line 245):

> Stay, dog, for thou shalt hear me.
> If heaven have any grievous plague in store
> Exceeding those that I can wish upon thee,
> O let them keep it till thy sins be ripe,
> And then hurl down their indignation
> On thee, the troubler of the poor world's peace! ...
> No sleep close up that deadly eye of thine,
> Unless it be while some tormenting dream
> Affrights thee with a hell of ugly devils!
> Thou elvish-marked, abortive, rooting hog!   (215-227)

The long dying fall of Clarence (I.iv).

Swiftly we move to Richard sending the murderers to Clarence, and the vivid scene of Clarence's dream and murder, which Shakespeare entirely invented. About to be killed on Richard's orders, Clarence clings to the illusion that his brother loves him. This is an ironic mistake when, even in his ghastly dream, Richard drowns him. Clarence's nightmare is a vision spoken in verse of particular quality, which has been called "doom music":

> As we paced along
> Upon the giddy footing of the hatches,
> Methought that Gloucester stumbled, and in falling
> Struck me, that thought to stay him, overboard
> Into the tumbling billows of the main.　　　(16-20)

So Clarence drowns:

> O Lord! Methought what pain it was to drown!
> What dreadful noise of water in mine ears!
> What sights of ugly death within mine eyes!
> Methoughts I saw a thousand fearful wracks;
> A thousand men that fishes gnawed upon;
> Wedges of gold, great anchors, heaps of pearl,
> Inestimable stones, unvalued jewels,
> All scattered in the bottom of the sea.　　　(21-28)

And he goes to hell —

> O then began the tempest to my soul!
> I passed, methought, the melancholy flood,
> With that sour ferryman which poets write of,
> Unto the kingdom of perpetual night.
> The first that there did greet my stranger soul
> Was my great father-in-law, renownèd Warwick,
> Who spake aloud, 'What scourge for perjury
> Can this dark monarchy afford false Clarence?'
> And so he vanished. Then came wandering by
> A shadow like an angel, with bright hair
> Dabbled in blood, and he shrieked out aloud
> 'Clarence is come — false, fleeting, perjured Clarence,
> That stabbed me in the field by Tewkesbury.
> Seize on him, Furies, take him unto torment!'　(44-57)

This is as fine a passage in that style as any in English: it leaves its solemn music tolling in the ears. Delivered with deep feeling, as by Sir John Gielgud in the Olivier film, it is unforgettable. The doom music of Richard's reign is reiterated by his victims with images of oceanic storms, drowning, and the black deeps of the sea. Clarence genuinely repents. He warns his killers of God's vengeance; they remind him that he is a murderer. The reluctant Second Murderer might still save Clarence by listening to his conscience; he tries to warn him: "Look behind you, my lord!" But Clarence, who fears death by drowning, is stuffed into a butt of malmsey wine.

The Second Movement

The rhythm of the play changes from a simple beat, as Richard almost inevitably conquers all, to a more complex form, as we follow Richard's plotting to get rid of the Queen's party and Hastings. From here on, Shakespeare dramatizes the history of only two years, from the death of Edward IV in 1483 to the battle of Bosworth Field in 1485. He continues to alter historic facts to heighten their effect.

> *The dying Edward IV tries to make peace among the lords; Richard announces Clarence's death (II.i).*

> *Clarence's children and the Duchess of York mourn. Edward IV dies (II.ii).*

> *London citizens discuss the issues (II.iii).*

> *Richard breaks the Queen's power, arresting Rivers, Grey and Vaughan (II.iv).*

> *The princes go to the Tower for "safekeeping" (III.i).*

> *Hastings denies Richard's claim to the throne (III.ii).*

> *Rivers, Grey, and Vaughan are executed (III.iii).*

> *Hastings is arrested (III.iv.79).*

Shakespeare opens the Movement with a surprise: the trumpets blare for a royal entry, but Edward IV does not enter in triumph. He is carried in on a bier, deathly sick. The aural symbol is contrasted with the visual fact. Richard creates a deadly little playlet: he promises friendship to the Queen's followers then suddenly reveals Clarence's death, implying they have caused it.

On Edward's death, Richard becomes Lord Protector of the young Edward V and his brother and puts them in the Tower. He imprisons and executes Rivers, Grey, and Vaughan. Hastings has supported Edward V too strongly, so Richard creates a playlet for him, greeting him cordially. Hastings says:

> I think there's never a man in Christendom
> Can lesser hide his love or hate than he,
> For by his face straight shall you know his heart.
> (III.iv.51-53)

This is so far from the truth that, shortly afterwards, Richard exclaims:

> Thou art a traitor.
> Off with his head! Now by Saint Paul I swear
> I will not dine until I see the same! (75-77)

Hastings speaks on his fall in the doom music:

> O momentary grace of mortal men,
> Which we more hunt for than the grace of God!
> Who builds his hope in air of your good looks
> Lives like a drunken sailor on a mast,
> Ready with every nod to tumble down
> Into the fatal bowels of the deep. (96-101)

Hastings' last words, "They smile at me who shortly shall be dead" (line 107), are prophetic. They foretell a parallel fall for Buckingham.

The Third Movement

Whereas we have been highly amused by Richard, now the rhythm changes and we find him very funny indeed in a macabre way. This broader time-beat begins at the death of Hastings and continues with Richard's pious act before the Lord Mayor and the citizens. An alternating pulse appears in the Lady Anne scene, and finally an ominous feeling steadily deepens the coronation scene. Taking his lead from medieval drama, Shakespeare juxtaposes uproarious fun with tragic seriousness, as Richard loses control of his "play-within-a-play" in IV.ii.

Hastings is executed. The princes in the Tower are declared illegitimate (III.iv.80-III.v).

Hastings' head is presented to Richard who, as an actor, seems sick with disillusionment as he delivers one of the most sardonic lines in the play: "So dear I loved the man that I must weep" (III.v.24).

Unlike the nobles in *Henry VI*, those we now meet would prefer not to go to war, civil or otherwise. Hastings, Buckingham, and the rest would rather be accomplices of the Protector than genuine villains. But Richard is no longer simply a ravaging boar; he has become so skilful at deceit that he can operate in a peaceful society and completely hide the hatreds he voiced in *3 Henry VI*. We in the audience know his wickedness, but the audience of his peers in the "play within the play" do not, at least not until it is too late. Cleverly, he is always removed from the murderous acts; in society he flashes his wit rather than his knife, which others wield on his behalf. The warrior of *3 Henry VI* is now a dramatist and, we feel, does not want to get his hands bloody. As far as the rest know, Richard is content to beg some good strawberries from Ely's garden — but he wants to look at Hastings' severed head before he dines! Only at the end of the play, as he wields his own sword in battle with his old savagery, do others — at least, those who are still alive — see him as the boar he really is.

With the help of Buckingham, the Lord Mayor of London requests that Richard become king (III.v-III.vii).

We now reach the funniest sequence in the play. Here we do not meet the cool, ironic, and sardonic dramatist-Richard of the earlier Movements. Now he is the actor-in-role, with Buckingham as an actor-sidecoach. They perform a splendid two-scene playlet which sandwiches a short scene for the two counterfeits to plot their playing: an amusing scenario to get the crown, with some magnificent comic fooling by the pair as they try to persuade the Lord Mayor and the London bourgeoisie that Richard is pious.

First, Richard appears with a group of clergy and presents himself as a highly respectable, non-libidinous man, an ideal Christian monarch for a morally decent England. The idea is almost beyond belief, and yet this is the subject of his playing in this outrageous scene.

Very cautious but half-convinced, the Lord Mayor next leads a delegation to suggest, tentatively, that Richard accept the crown. Richard makes a flamboyant entrance, flanked by two bishops and holding a prayer book — the role transforms him into a pious Christian prince. Once again, his playing is highly successful. Despite his seemingly profound reluctance, he is "persuaded" to be king by "overwhelming" public demand (Buckingham and Catesby cheer from behind the Lord Mayor).

Thus Richard becomes king with a legal title by hereditary succession, official request, and public acclaim. Yet the title is fraudulent, the official approval is merely a hesitant request by a puzzled Lord Mayor, and the public acclaim is simply one of the sidecoach Buckingham's contrivances. Then, having accepted the burden of reigning in the secular world, Richard turns to the bishops and leaves the stage with perfect serenity. "Come, let us to our holy work again" (III.vii.245).

One of my favourite roles was when I doubled the Lord Mayor with Clarence in the tour of the English Drama Group in 1950. The major requirement of the actor of the Lord Mayor is that he appear bewildered by the brilliant "actors" around him — as are Anne, Hastings, and the nobility. The Lord Mayor is not a clown, as he is often played; he is, after all, the chief officer of the city. If the great people of the realm are fooled by Richard-the-player, so is he. The scenes are not farcical, but they are broadly comic, to contrast with the coronation scene.

In his film, Olivier ended the Lord Mayor's sequence by swinging down from above on a rope, and he menacingly forced Buckingham to kneel and kiss his hand. This change was too early. As it was abrupt, it riveted us in our seats. But Shakespeare has carefully plotted this change in Richard's attitude to Buckingham to occur in the middle of the coronation scene.

Queen Elizabeth, the Duchess of York, and Anne are refused permission to visit the princes in the Tower, and when Anne is told she is to be crowned as Richard's queen, they all realize the danger to the princes (IV.i).

When Anne leaves to be crowned as Richard's queen, she goes to meet the curse she herself put on Richard's wife before he wooed and won her.

> *Richard now must make the crown secure, but he becomes increasingly hesitant. Buckingham has no enthusiasm to kill the princes and escapes before Richard can kill him. The princes are murdered in the Tower by Tyrrell. Anne dies (IV.ii-IV.iii).*

After the coronation, Richard ascends the throne, led by Buckingham, whose help he acknowledges:

> Thus high, by thy advice
> And thy assistance, is King Richard seated.   (IV.ii.3-4)

Richard then broaches the killing of the princes with Buckingham who goes away to think about it. Thus Buckingham makes himself one of the future victims of Richard, who, throwing him off with a snub, sends Tyrrell to murder them. Richmond has landed, and one by one, various lords desert Richard for him. Richard is beginning to lose control and become more uncertain.

Tyrrell reports to Richard the murder of the princes. As in *3 Henry VI* and *King John,* the murder of children is a crowning villainy which society must reject. Richard is contemptuous of Tyrrell's remorse, and greets him sardonically as "king Tyrrell" and "gentle Tyrrell." But Tyrrell's remorse is genuine. Before this moment, the frankness of Richard's dedication to evil had an amusing charm. But now the mood has changed: the pitilessness of his response to Tyrrell is horrifying. Richard's summing-up is brisk:

> The son of Clarence have I pent up close,
> His daughter meanly have I matched in marriage,
> The sons of Edward sleep in Abraham's bosom,
> And Anne my wife hath bid this world good night.
> (IV.iii.36-39)

But as Richmond plans to marry

> young Elizabeth, my brother's daughter,
> And by that knot looks proudly on the crown,
> To her go I, a jolly thriving wooer.   (41-43)

The Fourth Movement

The next Movement signals a major rhythmical change: Richard's fortunes ebb, and Richmond's flow. Richmond's army comes ever closer. Richard has little humour, and he cannot control events. His brilliance loses its fascination: the "moral holiday" created by the dramatist-Richard with his witty audacity and preposterous poses is at an end. He has lost two levels of meaning: no longer a successful dramatist or actor, now he is only himself as an actor-in-role.

> *In a long, choric lamentation scene of the two queens and the Duchess, there is a repetition of Margaret's curse with the curse of Richard's mother added (IV.iv.1-197) .*

So now prosperity begins to mellow
And drop into the rotten mouth of death.   (1-2)

This magnificent metaphor of decay, generated by the civil war, opens a great choric scene. Richard rises as a misshapen growth of a misshapen age, and prospers; at his greatest success God rids the land of a festering evil.

This is Margaret's most impressive scene. She is joined by Richard's mother, the Duchess of York, and the widowed Elizabeth. The three wronged and afflicted women sit on the earth to embark upon an elaborate ritual of lamentation — a formalized contrast with what has come before, and one which foreshadows the ghosts. The old Duchess of York bewails England's condition:

Brief abstract and record of tedious days,
Rest thy unrest on England's lawful earth,
Unlawfully made drunk with innocents' blood!   (28-30)

Margaret's passion for revenge reaches new heights: "Richard yet lives, hell's black intelligencer" (line 71), but she anticipates his terrible death:

Earth gapes, hell burns, fiends roar, saints pray,
To have him suddenly conveyed from hence.
Cancel his bond of life, dear God, I pray,
That I may live to say, 'The dog is dead.'   (75-78)

She bequeaths to Elizabeth grim instructions in the art of cursing:

Forbear to sleep the nights, and fast the days;
Compare dead happiness with living woe;

> Think that thy babes were sweeter than they were
> And he that slew them fouler than he is.
> Bettering thy loss makes the bad causer worse;
> Revolving this will teach thee how to curse.   (118-123)

Shakespeare is at his nearest to classic drama here. He has created a new variation on Seneca's spirit from another world howling for revenge. The revenge spirit is seen to be human as these three sad women wail. The scene is so antagonistic to realistic conventions that it is not surprising it was sometimes cut. Sir Henry Irving at first omitted it but later played it and was largely responsible for its acceptance by late Victorian audiences. Since that time, it has been accepted that the deep meanings of the play lie in such ritualistic scenes.

> *In a second wooing scene, Richard tries to arrange with
> Queen Elizabeth for a politically advantageous marriage
> with her daughter. But this fails: Elizabeth promises her
> daughter to Richmond (IV.iv.198-431).*

Shakespeare shows the subtle ways that Richard's failure here parodies his triumphant seduction of the Lady Anne. He repeats the arguments and poses that dazzled Anne but now with no success. Richard then stoops to lies and bribes. Because he is incapable of love, his suit is impossible. Used to dealing with human beings as objects, he tries to bargain with Elizabeth like a peddler: so many grandchildren weighed against so many children murdered — a commercial transaction of flesh and blood. But his cynical offers of profit are useless:

> If I did take the kingdom from your sons,
> To make amends I'll give it to your daughter;
> If I have killed the issue of your womb,
> To quicken your increase I will beget
> Mine issue of your blood upon your daughter ...
> Again shall you be mother to a king,
> And all the ruins of distressful times
> Repaired with double riches of content.
> What! We have many goodly days to see:
> The liquid drops of tears that you have shed
> Shall come again, transformed to orient pearl,
> Advantaging their love with interest
> Of ten times double gain of happiness.   (294-324)

Desperate and bankrupt, he gives a promissory note that falls
due at Bosworth field:

> As I intend to prosper and repent,
> So thrive I in my dangerous affairs
> Of hostile arms! Myself myself confound!
> Heaven and fortune bar me happy hours!
> Day, yield me not thy light, nor, night, thy rest!
> Be opposite all planets of good luck
> To my proceedings if, with dear heart's love,
> Immaculate devotion, holy thoughts,
> I tender not thy beauteous princely daughter! (397-405)

The destructive sea appears again in Elizabeth's lines:

> But that still use of grief makes wild grief tame,
> My tongue should to thy ears not name my boys
> Till that my nails were anchored in thine eyes;
> And I, in such a desperate bay of death,
> Like a poor bark of sails and tackling reft,
> Rush all to pieces on thy rocky bosom.   (230-235)

The ship, anchors, and eyes from Clarence's dream reappear,
and the "bay of death" is the boar's.

This long scene is often edited, or even cut, in production.
Cutting it is no solution, because the symmetry with the Lady
Anne scene is part of the play's inherent structure. Editors,
however, do have an argument: it is excessively long, even con-
sidering the balance with I.ii, as well as the nature of
Elizabethan staging.

> *Richmond sails for England; Buckingham raises a force to
> join him. Buckingham is captured. Richmond lands with
> a "mighty power" (IV.iv.432-540).*

> *Richmond marches on London. Many lords join him;
> Elizabeth consents to her daughter's marriage to him
> (IV.v).*

> *Buckingham dies. (V.i).*

Richard is disintegrating. No longer a player or dramatist, as
his true self he is desperate: he orders Catesby to go to the Duke
of Norfolk and then forgets to tell him why; he commands
Ratcliffe to go to Salisbury and then changes his mind; and he

strikes a messenger before he learns his news, which turns out to be favourable. The great actor is forgetting his lines.

Buckingham disregarded Margaret's warning about Richard (I.iii). He created his own nemesis when he prayed that if ever he harmed Queen Elizabeth or her family God might punish him with hate where he expected most love (II.i). He joined the plot against her and her sons, and gained the crown for Richard, for whom he became "my other self, my counsel's consistory" (II.ii.151). Now he hesitates before consenting to the murder of the princes in the Tower, so when he claims the earldom of Hereford, promised him earlier, he gets a brutal snub: "I am not in the giving vein to-day" (IV.ii.115). Richard's reward for him is death. In the doom music which leads to our pity for his fall, Buckingham acknowledges its justice and recognizes his errors.

The Fifth Movement

Richard III dies for his evil acts. Such is God's justice, to leave no unrepentant wickedness unpunished, as Holinshed says. God uses Richard as a scourge to punish the sins of others and then raises up Richmond to remove "one that hath ever been God's enemy." Thus order may be restored to a troubled realm. In the death-and-resurrection tradition, what is complete must die so that what is potential can live.

At Bosworth, Richmond and his forces arrive (V.ii).

The two armies camp down for the night, ready for battle in the morning. Richard has a ghostly dream (V.iii).
On the eve of the Battle of Bosworth, Richard confesses,
I have not that alacrity of spirit
Nor cheer of mind that I was wont to have. (V.iii.73-74)
Richard and Richmond, in a stylized sequence, withdraw to their tents and prepare for sleep. As they share the same stage it is usual to place their tents on either side, contrasted by lighting and coloured banners.

Richard's dream-prologue to the battle is a major change by Shakespeare from Holinshed's *Chronicles* where Richard dreams of terrible devils. Richard's nightmare now is a medieval vision of the souls of those he has murdered. Each blesses Richmond's enterprise and curses Richard: Prince Edward; Henry VI; Clarence; Rivers, Grey, and Vaughan; Hastings; Buckingham; the two young princes; and wretched Anne. It is the ultimate irony that Richard, the consummate "false actor," should at last deceive and confound himself. He cries out in the real world the fears that beset him in the dream world:

> Give me another horse! Bind up my wounds!
> Have mercy, Jesu!   (178-179)

He is more frightened by the images of his own mind than by Richmond's army. The ghosts make Richard bear witness against himself, in a remarkable double dialogue, as he wakes:

> What do I fear? Myself? There's none else by.
> Richard loves Richard: that is, I am I.
> Is there a murderer here? No. Yes, I am.
> Then fly. What, from myself? Great reason why —
> Lest I revenge. Myself upon myself?
> Alack, I love myself. Wherefore? For any good
> That I myself have done unto myself?
> O no! Alas, I rather hate myself
> For hateful deeds committed by myself.
> I am a villain. Yet I lie, I am not.   (183-192)

The broken phrases show that Richard's personality is under attack, an important indicator for the actor. The nightmare is a ritual of excommunication: he is cast out by the dead, as by the living, when each ghost cries, "Despair and die!" Richard looks into himself with horror: he has cut himself off from humanity, and for the first time he is frightened:

> I shall despair. There is no creature loves me;
> And if I die, no soul will pity me.   (201-202)

But he is unrepentant in the morning and reaffirms his principles:

> Let not our babbling dreams affright our souls;
> Conscience is but a word that cowards use,
> Devised at first to keep the strong in awe.
> Our strong arms be our conscience, swords our law!
>   (309-312)

*In the Battle of Bosworth, Richard's forces are depleted by
many defections. In the confusion, Richard is forced to
fight on his feet before he is killed. Richmond (the future
Henry VII) will unite the realm (V.iv-V.v).*

Richard pulls himself together and takes on the enemy
courageously. He regains his equilibrium, fighting on foot
against overwhelming odds:

> I think there be six Richmonds in the field;
> Five have I slain today instead of him.
> A horse! a horse! my kingdom for a horse!   (V.iv.11-13)

He dies a soldier's death: a heroic but invidious end that is a
paradox — his only possible fulfillment. With his death, the
demands for vengeance made by Queen Margaret are met.

On stage, the Battle of Bosworth is not only a dramatic act.
It also re-creates the ancient ritual battle (Winter vs. Summer)
that brings power. When Richmond and Richard share the
stage, ritual opposites confront each other: good vs. evil, love
vs. hate, and society vs. anti-social individualism. Evil loses and
good wins — "The king is dead! long live the king!" — and the
War of the Roses is finally over. Richard became England's
scourge by repaying murder with murder and settling all the
criminal accounts of the past civil war except his own. With perfect justice, he is his own nemesis. At Bosworth he is the only
one left with bloody hands: a savage boar alone ready for sacrifice, a scapegoat laden with all the sins of his time. Englishmen
unite to hunt down their enemy: a communal ritual of peace-
loving men to restore society.

Richmond is the one chosen to answer the call of outraged
humanity. But he has no role in this play until its end. His victory has nothing to do with who he is; it is about what he represents. He is virtually an abstraction, with little characterization,
who is to unify the country in peace. In *3 Henry VI* Henry
blessed a youth whom he points to as England's hope, and the
ghost of Henry recalls this prophecy in *Richard III:*

> Virtuous and holy, be thou conqueror!
> Harry, that prophesied thou shouldst be king,
> Doth comfort thee in thy sleep; live, and flourish!
>   (V.iii.129-131)

Richmond, virtuous and holy, is an agent of God:

O thou whose captain I account myself,
Look on my forces with a gracious eye.   (V.iii.109-110)
There is no emphasis placed on Richmond's military prowess; indeed, only a stage direction in the last scene tells us that he kills Richard in combat. Then Richmond, soon to be crowned Henry VII, announces the reuniting of York and Lancaster through his marriage with Elizabeth, daughter of Edward IV:
And let their heirs, God, if Thy will be so,
Enrich the time to come with smooth-faced peace,
With smiling plenty, and fair prosperous days!
(V.v.32-34)

FORM

What kind of play is *Richard III*? Is it, as Shakespeare calls it, "a tragedy"? Yet there is no hero. As the vendetta of York and Lancaster continues, it might be "a revenge tragedy." Or, as it concerns the life and death of a tyrant, is it a Seneca-type tragedy? It is also very amusing: Richard is witty and has a sardonic humour, at least until he becomes king. *Richard III* is not just "a history play." Is it a melodrama? Richard is an exaggerated villain. The triumph of right is without the improbability one sees in melodrama. In fact, does *Richard III* belong to any one genre?

The play has a unique kind of tragic quality: the tragedy of people, a family, a nation, of society as a whole, where right triumphs as the probable result of human actions. It is also ironic: Richard, by destroying others, destroys himself. He rises steadily until his coronation, when he orders the murder of his nephews. From then on, he turns friends to enemies until "he hath no friends but what are friends for fear" (V.ii.20).

But Richard does not have the inner conflict of Macbeth, who inspires pity as well as fear. We have no pity for Richard. To begin with, we have more amusement than pity for him. The play is tragic because, by the end, we in the audience have had a tragic experience: retributive justice strikes down Richard and the total Plantagenet family. Shakespeare also shows how the people of England suffered from tyranny and civil war, when the brother blindly shed the brother's blood. The play ends with a prayer that England may live in peace.

If the genre of the play is imprecise, its structure is paradoxically both highly formal and daring.

STRUCTURE

Richard III is Shakespeare's most formally structured play. It builds so far on the symmetry of *3 Henry VI* that he never wrote anything like it again, presumably because he became aware of its limitations. It has a multiple structure, the strands of which are always difficult for a dramatist to manipulate. We have seen that the play has five Movements with the major climax at the coronation scene. *Thus the first and fundamental structure is the villainous theatrical career of Richard: the linear, or horizontal, framework within which the other structures are set.* Shakespeare amplifies Richard's life by creating a fascinating creature surrounded by people who are less interesting than he, and in a memorable and awesome artistic structure. He creates the longest night of the Plantagenets, whose rule is a terrifying nightmare, a living hell in which no one knows where Richard will strike next. Shakespeare structures a sprawling action of great length, which unfolds progressively with threats, dire prophecies, violence, murder, choric laments, medieval moralizing, accusing ghosts and, hanging over everyone, the twisted shadow of Richard — chilling and deadly.

Shakespeare weaves into his horizontal framework various vertical structures. *The second structure consists of the various fresh discoveries of political and moral reality.* These discoveries tumble over each other. Thus the opening scene (Clarence goes to his death) demonstrates how little familial love means in a world of *realpolitik*. Then quickly we are swept into the scene with the Lady Anne, where we identify with her moral dilemmas as she faces political and personal reality. Throughout the play, both characters and audience face moral and political issues of great moment.

The vertical structure of these first two scenes pushes the linear framework ahead at a swift rate, foregrounding important political and moral issues which, in their contrasts, are central to the play. Indeed, *contrast is the third structure.* All of Shakespeare's plays mix contrasting forces but nowhere else with such extremes and (given Richard's sharp mind) with such speed as in this play. In the early scenes we realize that the "winter of our discontent" results in vicious acts. The play, like its central figure, is conceived in contrary forces: blood and death vs. ribald wit; gothic shapes vs. Renaissance energies; tragic pathos vs. historical narrative; the wailing of grief-stricken women vs. a high-spirited comedian; and Senecan gloom vs. ironic comedy.

Amid these general contraries run several specific and important contrasts which the director must note. The contrast between pity and terror occurs throughout. Richard epitomizes terror. No one pities Richard, but we often pity those who suffer at his hands.

Some important scenes are structured in *triple contrasts* rather than pairs. The deaths of Edward and Clarence leave three generations (mother, wife, and children) desolate — and Shakespeare emphasizes this twice. Just prior to the coronation, there is a triple lament by the old Duchess of York, Anne, and Queen Elizabeth. After the murderers of the two boys tell of their deaths, a chorus of grief rises in the laments of their mother, their grandmother, and Queen Margaret. These scenes intensify emotion by a triple pattern, as though the sorrow was too great to be expressed by only one person. Other responses of pity to Richard's terror are even more complex. Did Shakespeare realize that pity and terror are the focus of Aristotle's theory of tragic catharsis?

The contrast created by analogy creates significant meaning, and the audience can understand the meaning unconsciously. The dynamic of analogy is the relation of similarity and difference: two cases that are similar also differ from one another. For example, the killing of the princes is similar to, but different from, the Massacre of the Innocents, and the mother of the princes is both like and unlike Rachel weeping for her children. In a more subtle fashion, there are many images that hint at analogy: "The royal tree hath left us royal fruit" (III.vii.166) hints at the fecundity of the ancient religions and Christianity to which Richard stands opposed.

The contrast created by symbols is an extreme kind of analogy. Like so many Shakespearean works, *Richard III* contrasts two primary themes: power and love. Power for Shakespeare is often symbolized by the crown, which here is used for evil until

Richmond obtains it at Bosworth. Then it is used for good. The
theme of love creates three kinds of symbols:

[1]   The theme of the loved dead.

Richard does not wish to hear the voice of
Margaret: it prophesies his doom. She calls up the
ghosts in the night before Bosworth — the shades of
Margaret's twisted version of love. The curse stood for
retributive justice in orthodox Tudor thinking, but in
the play it means much more. Margaret represents
the House of Lancaster, now the walking dead who
will haunt the butcher of the House of York. She
memorializes the long civil war and the slaughter of
those she has loved.

[2]   The theme of empathy for those suffering at
Richard's hands.

This theme has many facets in *Richard III*. While
Anne expresses her love for her dead husband and
her love for her cousins, the princes in the Tower, she
contrasts this love with hatred of Richard and the
crown.

[3]   The theme of the potential love of the Tudors for the
land and its people.

The few expressions of religious love contrast with
Richard's lust for the crown. It is Richmond, who, in
defeating Richard and marrying Elizabeth, expects to
unite the land in love and

Enrich the time to come with smooth-faced peace,
With smiling plenty, and fair prosperous days!

(V.v.33-34)

THE THEATRICAL KING

Richard makes us remember that we are in a playhouse witnessing a theatrical performance. He dominates the play: he is in
most of the scenes, his shadow hangs over the rest, and he has
nearly a third of the lines in Shakespeare's longest play except
Hamlet. Richard overwhelms us. In the first of Shakespeare's
truly great roles, his utter theatricality needs no apology. A dis-
simulator in *3 Henry VI*, here he is an urbane masquerader, a
supreme individualist. The others, except Margaret, cannot

fathom him, and he "plays" them like fish on a line. Even after Richmond appears, Richard is the only antagonist worthy of himself; in the end, he even has to play his own accuser.

Shakespeare adds to his basic idea of Richard three older performers: the Vice, the Actor, and the Machiavellian. First, as Richard himself tells us (III.i.82-83), he is the Vice: the medieval stage dissembler and hypocrite, a counterfeit who takes the audience into his confidence. Shakespeare used the Richard of More's *History* who was a "deep dissimuler," a master of many roles, similar to the Vice. But when Richard acts "the devil" (I.iii.337), "the maid's part" (III.vii.50), "the eavesdropper" (V.iii.222), and other roles, they acquire a sinister significance. Second is the Actor. Accused of being counterfeits by puritanical Elizabethans, professional actors put on roles to hide their real personalities from the audience. Shakespeare raises this issue in many plays, so it clearly concerns him greatly. As "Vice-actors," Richard and Buckingham fully realize they are counterfeits:

> RICHARD: Come cousin, canst thou quake and change
> thy colour,
> Murder thy breath in middle of a word,
> And then again begin, and stop again,
> As if thou were distraught and mad with
> terror?
>
> BUCK.: Tut, I can counterfeit the deep tragedian,
> Speak and look back, and pry on every side,
> Tremble and start at wagging of a straw;
> Intending deep suspicion.   (III.v.1-8)

Third, Shakespeare adds the notion of the Machiavellian who uses deceit and simulation to achieve personal power. The childish trust of his nephews provokes the old Duchess of York into a bitter exclamation against Richard the Machiavellian actor:

> Ah, that deceit should steal such gentle shape,
> And with a virtuous visor hide deep vice!   (II.ii.27-28)

The play tests the deeper moral implications of Machiavellianism. Richard's true enemy is not Richmond but the moral force within the responses of Clarence's murderers, Tyrrell, and Richard's own suppressed humanity which suddenly, but briefly, surfaces late in the play (V.iii.178-207).

Shakespeare weaves these three elements into a unique Richard who sees his vicious crimes as sport and shares the sardonic fun with us. Richard has an artist's delight in his craft; and he has a supporting actor, Buckingham, to perform deceiving playlets, who comments slyly,

> Had you not come upon your cue, my lord,
> William Lord Hastings had pronounced your part —
> I mean, your voice for crowning of the King. (III.iv.26-28)

Richard is not a simple hypocrite who lets us in on secrets. He uses specific performance techniques to show us his own play and his consummate acting: in his "super-asides," or his chuckling private jokes, made to "myself alone" — almost miniature soliloquies; or in his real asides which nudge the audience's attention, as when he receives his mother's blessing —

> Amen! And make me die a good old man!
> That is the butt end of a mother's blessing;
> I marvel that her grace did leave it out.   (II.ii.109-111)

As the Londoners believe that Richard must be persuaded to be king, Buckingham pretends to lose patience, with, "Zounds, I'll entreat no more," and the pious Richard says, "O, do not swear, my lord of Buckingham" (III.vii.219). Like *Hamlet*, *Richard III* asserts the power of the human actor over other people. Richard deceives almost everyone by the power of illusion, as he says in *3 Henry VI* (III.ii.182-195), and sometimes seems bewildered by the extent of his own power:

> And I no friends to back my suit at all
> But the plain devil and dissembling looks ...
>
> (I.ii.235-236)

How far is Richard believed by the others in the play? The point is, they all act as though they believe him: everyone (but his trusting brothers) knows his real character and fears him. But in a corrupt world no one dare risk questioning him. Also watching an actor or a play has the power of revealing the truth ("The play's the thing," says Hamlet, "Wherein I'll catch the conscience of the king"). Often, watching a performance brings violence. Immediately after the ambiguous word "scene" comes:

> DUCHESS: What means this scene of rude impatience?
> QUEEN: To make an act of tragic violence.
>
> (II.ii.38-39)

Paradoxically, Richard is part Devil and part the agent of God. He is a wicked villain, but his success as an actor makes fiction attractive, and his fiendish but clownish humour makes evil amusing.

> And thus I clothe my naked villainy
> With odd old ends stolen forth of Holy Writ,
> And seem a saint, when most I play the devil.
>
> (I.iii.335-337)

In the Tudor view he is God's agent in a predetermined plan of divine retribution. He is the "scourge of God," a divine avenger on the wicked. As paradox, he is both the logical outcome of his times and a scapegoat rejected by society. But Richard is no stereotype. If he performs "fictions," they have bloodcurdling results. We laugh at his ingenuity, yet we also feel guilty because his fictions suggest ourselves and people that we know.

Shakespeare's idea of acting in Richard III is an advance on that in *Henry VI*. In *Richard III*, what a person *plays* (his role) is who he *is*. His role affects his speech. Richard has his own way of talking: he can speak like others to deceive them; and he can combine his own way with others' to parody them, as with "Simple plain Clarence" (I.i.118-120). Richard improvises so well that we almost want him to win, until IV.ii, where his change begins: the brilliant improviser cannot act a scripted role. He ascends the throne with a royal ceremony that stresses the external nature of kingship — a script formed by convention. For the first time he must act in a moral structure. His task as a player alters. At once, the great actor becomes an amateur and fails. When he tries to repeat Anne's wooing for Elizabeth's daughter he fails and threatens. When he forgets to send a message with a messenger at Bosworth, it is as if he has forgotten his lines. Richard is left to improvise with himself:

> I am a villain. Yet I lie, I am not.
> Fool, of thyself speak well. Fool, do not flatter.
> My conscience hath a thousand several tongues,
> And every tongue brings in a several tale,
> And every tale condemns me for a villain. (V.iii.192-196)

Richard's last role is that of his own accuser.

But Richard is more than an actor. He relates to us as a dramatist of a "play within a play." As an artist in evil, he literally plots the performance which he dominates from beginning to end. To others, his inner reality is invisible, but he reminds the audience of both his intentions and his acting ability. Thus he plays the bluff, plain Englishman, shocked at ambitious deceivers, before the Queen's relations:

> Because I cannot flatter and look fair,
> Smile in men's faces, smooth, deceive, and cog,
> Duck with French nods and apish courtesy,
> I must be held a rancorous enemy.
> Cannot a plain man live and think no harm
> But thus his simple truth must be abused
> With silken, sly, insinuating Jacks?   (I.iii.47-53)

He turns to the audience:

> But then I sigh, and, with a piece of Scripture,
> Tell them that God bids us do good for evil.
>   (I.iii.333-334)

Like *The Spanish Tragedy, Richard III* is a play dominated by the image of the world as a stage. But Kyd is less subtle than Shakespeare, who only *suggests* a "play within the play," focusing on the great actor as puppeteer. The idea that life imitates the theatre is built into the play. Richard is, as Henry VI realized too late, devoted to performing in real life the scenes of death *(3 Henry VI* V.vi.10). Margaret says that, when Prince Edward was killed by York's sons, several others were "the beholders of this frantic play" (IV.iv.68). The comparison of life with the drama rises naturally from the context and is both convincing and moving.

Richard III is Shakespeare's first major creation of the Player King, an image he develops throughout his career, the king who is aware that he is acting a regal role. Richard, Claudius, Macbeth, Lear, Richard II, and Henry IV are all imperfect kings; there is a clash between the person and the part he is playing. The clash occurs at Richard's coronation and evokes the image of a flawed actor and a flawed king. What makes him different from the other Player Kings is the theatrical imagery that surrounds him. Shakespeare also introduces the idea of the Player Queen, a woman whose regal dignity is an idle show with no meaning. Margaret recalls that she always regarded her rival as a queen without a title to the crown:

> I called thee then vain flourish of my fortune;
> I called thee then poor shadow, painted queen,

> The presentation of but what I was,
> The flattering index of a direful pageant ...
> A sign of dignity, a breath, a bubble,
> A queen in jest, only to fill the scene.   (IV.iv.82-91)

In *The Winter's Tale*, the Player Queen re-appears, but in a different way. Richard also foreshadows the actor-villains of the later plays: Claudius, Macbeth, Edmund and Iago. Yet Richard is so much part of the theatre that he shows the power of the actor more than of treachery and evil.

Only in *Macbeth* do the words "tyrant" and "tyranny" appear more frequently. Richard is Shakespeare's version of a tyrant. The sense of horror continues after the murder. Tyrrell says -

> The tyrannous and bloody act is done,
> The most arch deed of piteous massacre
> That ever yet this land was guilty of.   (IV.iii.1-3)

The description of the murderers, who "wept like to children in their death's sad story" (IV.iii.8), and their account of the children's death is pathetic. So is the scene of lamentation of the queens and the Duchess. Margaret prays for one more killing, that of Richard, that she "may live to say, 'The dog is dead'" (IV.iv.78). The Tudor myth requires that Richard is branded a tyrant and that his removal is seen as an act of divine providence and justice. The many images linked to him (e.g., "foul devil," "the son of hell," "thou'st made this happy earth thy hell") make him almost satanic. Shakespeare takes the political meaning of the play well beyond the Providence of his historical sources.

Richard links past and present: he brings the vendettas of the past and makes them live in the present tense. The worst offence of the Colley Cibber version of the play is that it detaches the present from the past. Richard as tyrant has brought about some interesting parallels. Sir Donald Wolfit suggested Hitler in his make-up as Richard, and in 1811 Richard's character was thought to have gained credibility through a comparison with Napoleon.

VICTIMS AND A PUPPET

In the play, Richmond is a puppet, while everyone else is drowning or choking in the black depths, the ocean, the perpetual night of Richard's reign. No characters are developed further than to interact with him. They all speak the language of conventional morality, which Richard does not.

Clarence thinks he has been sent to the Tower by the influence of the Queen's party. He believes Richard's worried "We are not safe, Clarence; we are not safe," and cannot see the ironic joke; he has no idea that he has been first on Richard's list since *3 Henry VI* (V.vi). "Simple" Clarence, a villain, repents, but the murderers' hypocritical comments are full of sardonic humour. The joke, however, is not funny. The more reluctant of the assassins, full of remorse, will have none of the reward. Hastings and Buckingham think themselves Richard's accomplices, not his puppets. They betray themselves, Hastings by revenge and pride, Buckingham by greed and ambition. We respect Hastings for being true to the princes, and we are amused by Buckingham's role playing, but there is an ironic justice in their fates. Anne cannot match Richard's brutal will except with words, not violence:

> Nay, do not pause; for I did kill King Henry —
> But 'twas thy beauty that provokèd me,
> Nay, now dispatch; 'twas I that stabbed young Edward —
> But 'twas thy heavenly face that set me on.
> *[She falls the sword.]*
> Take up the sword again, or take up me.   (I.ii.179-183)

Terrified and humiliated, the best she can say is, "I would I knew your heart." Her change is sudden because she does not know what else to do.

The second wooing scene, traditionally cut in performance, is a necessity; Richard must win Elizabeth's daughter to stabilize his reign. He still thinks he is a jolly, thriving wooer, but he is an unsuccessful actor. Unlike Anne, Elizabeth knows his purposes — Margaret has trained her. This scene is the reverse of the first: she has Richard's former strength, while he is vulnerable. Elizabeth does to Richard what he did to Anne.

Not only Richmond is a symbol of England's historical destiny. So is Margaret, Reignier's daughter once picked up on a battlefield by Suffolk and married to the weak husband, Henry VI. In the *Henry VI* plays, Margaret committed atrocities that are now in the dim past. Here she is old Queen Margaret, the venerable "she-wolf of France," the prophetic voice of an avenging nemesis calling divine retribution down on Richard. Like a Senecan Fury shrieking out of hell, she is a bitter, passionate woman isolated by her warped emotions, wanting an eye for an eye. She prays to a pitiless deity whose "justice" is a horror:

> O upright, just, and true-disposing God,
> How do I thank Thee that this carnal cur [Richard]
> Preys on the issue of his mother's body
> And makes her pew-fellow with others' moan!
> (IV.iv.55-58)

Where Richard speaks of Elizabeth's children as merchandise, Margaret balances the murder of children like counting old sacks. When the Duchess of York says she wept for Margaret's losses, she continues her ghastly sums:

> Bear with me! I am hungry for revenge,
> And now I cloy me with beholding it.
> Thy Edward he is dead, that killed my Edward;
> Thy other Edward dead, to quit my Edward;
> Young York he is but boot [a measure], because both they
> Matched not the high perfection of my loss. (IV.iv.61-66)

Her function is to thunder as a prophetess sent to warn that no sinner can escape his doom. Her cry for revenge is the direct antithesis of Richmond's appeal for reconciliation, the greater lesson of mercy so necessary to England's future. She is stuck in the past, but he looks to the future.

Richmond, however, is a puppet compared with Richard, who is alive and vital, enjoying life. Richmond is a cipher with no voice of his own. His speeches sound conventionally pious, but, juxtaposed against Richard's, they have a genuine power. Richmond deliberately avoids the issue of the Tudor claim to the succession, and his own position as "rebel," in his oration to his army. He pictures the battle against Richard as self-defence: Englishmen protect their homes and families against the ravening boar. *In terms of the play,* Richmond has no need to make his claim to the throne, because his "legitimacy" is moral, not genealogical. His mission is to deliver England from both Richard's tyranny and the hatreds of the past, including Margaret's thirst for vengeance. Richmond is a spiritual leader who brings mercy to England and, in contrast to Richard, Richmond enjoys "the sweetest sleep, and fairest-boding dreams" (V.iii.228).

VERSE

The blank verse of *Richard III* is not subtle, but its careful design contributes to its power. It has a strong emphatic rhythm. The pause at the end of the line, or sometimes of two lines (I.i.1-13), lets the actor dwell on the meaning with clarity and force.

Shakespeare often builds soliloquies in quatrains (four-line groups), as in the first soliloquy (expanded twice to five lines and once to six) and the soliloquies that begin and end the second scene of Act I (also with three or five lines). Dialogues vary. Here Shakespeare uses *stichomythia:* single line set against single line, as in Richard's word duels: with Anne in Act I scene ii, and Elizabeth in Act IV scene iv. One speaker takes from the other the same number of syllables and the maximum number of the same words (or their logical opposites) to repeat the sentence form as nearly as possible. The Tudors saw such verbal devices as equivalent to skills they admired in Seneca (as T.S. Eliot pointed out).*

> ANNE: I would I knew thy heart.
> RICHARD: 'Tis figured in my tongue.
> ANNE: I fear me both are false.
> RICHARD: Then never was man true.   (I.ii.192-195)

Those reversals (heart-tongue; false-true) create dramatic irony: patterned wit quickly inverted to parallel the irony of the plot.

Richard's mind is more rhetorical than poetic. As he loses his power his rhetoric grows as artificial as that of others. The opening scene is rich in antitheses: war-peace, lover-villain, etc. Anne expresses her grief (I.ii) by repetition and parallelism: "Set down, set down," "bloodless ... blood," "if ever he have child ... if ever he have wife." Margaret curses with power by repeated exclamations and key words (curse, death); paradoxical antithesis ("Dead life, blind sight, poor mortal living ghost"); repeated questions ("Where is thy husband now? Where be thy brothers?" IV.ii); and emphatic parallels (IV.iv.20-21, 40-46, 98-104).

---

* Eliot (1932) 138.

There are continuous iterations and parallelisms for dramatic effect. The two wooing scenes are the simplest example. The lamentation scenes, however, can prove difficult for modern directors. They often appear to be merely genealogical. For example, Queen Margaret says:

> I had an Edward, till a Richard killed him;
> I had a Harry, till a Richard killed him:
> Thou hadst an Edward, till a Richard killed him;
> Thou hadst a Richard, till a Richard killed him.
>
> (IV.iv.40-43)

Who is being talked about? (The last two are the princes in the Tower, so Elizabeth is being addressed). The stiffly formal manipulation of the echoing phrase and sequence of words is not intended to be realistic; it indicates a ritualization of the staging to parallel the language. Although the sense of the past evoked in these choric and ritual scenes is necessary to the play, we cannot expect modern audiences to sort out current intrigues while they make sense of references to earlier events. Elizabethans would also have been confused. What matters is that the audience knows that *someone* did *something* in the past, and the director and actor know what.

Richard III shows Shakespeare enjoying his mastery over language, though he has not yet learned how to conceal his art.

THE TWISTED PARADOX

One reason *Richard III* was an enormous success when it was first performed was that it was daring. Tudor tradition said that Richard was a paradox, a devilish tyrant who had to be overthrown, and God's avenger on the accursed — an evil being who deserved punishment. But Shakespeare gives the paradox a twist by making Richard a *comic* villain. His "gallows" humour and his comic irreverences undermine proper Tudor principles. For most of the play we are on his side; we enjoy him for himself, not for religious or philosophic reasons. In his deadly practical joking, the physically deformed exposes intellectual and moral deformities. The play's unity *is* the paradox. It constantly displays inversions, verbal patterns, actions, irony, intentions, expectations, and the false-true in the histrionic character. Richard *is* a paradox. He is an anti-hero. We both hate him and love him, and we feel guilty about doing so.

Richard is also the living embodiment of *realpolitik*. He seizes and uses power for purely selfish ends; he deserves to suffer the worst horrors. But Richard, in addition, is the underdog who fights his way to the top, one man against the world. The climb to power is a deadly one — deadly to him, and deadly to anyone who stands in his way. He scrambles over their bodies to reach the crown.

There remains the question of laughter. In such a horrifying play, what kind of laughter does Richard raise? His asides about Clarence are mordant rather than side-splitting, but his response to his mother's blessing, if timed well (as with Brian Bedford at Stratford, Ontario), is uproarious, and the scenes with the Lord Mayor are comic delights.

Among famous modern Richards, two were slow villains: Balliol Holloway was somewhat over-serious in the part while Wolfit was a little too melodramatic. José Ferrer at New York City Center in 1953 made us laugh and shudder at the same time. Brian Bedford emphasized the actor-Richard with great distance from the roles he took in the playlets. Olivier on stage in his early performances did not produce the mordant and macabre laughter he obtained in the film. If one of the tests of a great role is the variety of interpretation it allows, then Richard III is one of the finest.

KING JOHN

A PLAY FOR DISCOVERY

Unlike the plays of the *Henry VI* trilogy, *King John* has yet to be "discovered" in our century. A recent random sample of playgoers at the Stratford Ontario Festival showed that this was the least known of Shakespeare's plays. Yet *King John* is a remarkable achievement for a young dramatist. It is a highly sophisticated, bitter, and even brutal story of the evils of political corruption, with a significant message for today.

It is also a daring experiment in a new dramatic form. Shakespeare continually creates new forms, but here he is very brave. Unlike typical heroes and heroines, his major characters change swiftly and often do the unexpected, and our responses to them alter during the play.

These innovations may explain why *King John* was not liked in the theatre of earlier times. But the lack of modern interest in the play is puzzling. I cannot believe that, as Sir Donald Wolfit once said privately, it is not popular today because it uses the term "bastard" as a proper noun. In performance, the play has a strong appeal. Unlike the Elizabethans, we expect to meet radical change quite regularly: our newspapers and newscasts are full of the political ups and downs of our fellow citizens, and we expect people to change and grow. But the effect of these changes in the playhouse is curious, because we learn *not* to identify with the characters. We distance ourselves from them and begin to think intellectually about the issues they address.* As today's audiences do not know the historical details of *King John,* it will help if the director makes the story line very clear.

---

* This distancing has only surface similarities with Brecht's V-Effekt.

King John is not Shakespeare's best work, but it would have made the reputation of any one else. Faulconbridge is a great role, and the play has memorable scenes, majestic verse, highly theatrical moments, a surprise ending, and glorious opportunities for actors. Typically, Colley Cibber cut whole sections and added others in his version (1745). Patriotic speeches were added in the Napoleonic period, when it was played by John Philip Kemble, his brother Charles, and Mrs. Siddons (1804).

In the nineteenth century it was not often staged, although Macready restored much of Shakespeare's text. An archeological tradition began in 1823, when Planché's production emphasized setting the play lavishly, with historic accuracy. This sumptuousness was repeated in the productions of Charles Kean and, in 1899, by Beerbohm Tree. In another tradition, Barry Sullivan played Faulconbridge as loutish and rustic (1866). Mrs. Cibber, Mrs. Siddons, and Helen Faucit all "showcased" Constance during their careers.

King John has rarely been produced in the twentieth century. Sir Ralph Richardson played Faulconbridge in the Sullivan manner (1931), and Sir Donald Wolfit brilliantly performed the title role on television (BBC TV, 1952). One of the most interesting productions was Douglas Seale's at Stratford-upon-Avon (1957) with Robert Harris as King John and Alec Clunes as a curiously sedate Faulconbridge. Surprisingly, the play has achieved little success in the theatre since then.*

A DOUBLE TEXT

The text is controversial. *King John* was first published in the 1623 *Folio*, still the only substantive text. Shakespeare may have written it between 1588 and a possible revision in 1594. It is closely linked to *The Troublesome Raigne of John, King of England...*, a two-part anonymous play.

In my view, the latter was probably a pirated edition or bad quarto of *King John,* since, in performance, the two scripts are remarkably alike. If so, the date of *King John* may be 1591 or earlier. But for most scholars King John was based on *The*

---

* For theatre history, see Sprague (1944, 1953, 1964), and Sprague and Trewin (1970).

Troublesome Raigne, written by someone else. Thus they believe that Shakespeare's play was written between 1591, when *The Troublesome Raigne* was published, and 1598 when Francis Meres mentioned *King John.* In the earlier play, John is the rightful king, and Faulconbridge's role is thinly written. When we perform the two plays, however, we discover some remarkable parallels. The plots are alike in the first three acts, and only a little less so in the last two. Their language is similar. There are line-by-line differences, but their substance and the order of the speeches are alike, and the people interact in the same way.

In the earlier play, John is the anti-papal hero, as he was in John Bale's play, *Kynge Johan,* and Foxe's *Book of Martyrs.* Shakespeare shifts away from one religious view. The heroic John of *The Troublesome Raigne* could not order the torture of an innocent child as the sinister figure in *King John* does. Probably Shakespeare learned from performances of the earlier play and made changes to King John. The weaknesses of the earlier play become *King John*'s strengths. *The Troublesome Raigne* ends:

> Let England live but true within itself,
> And all the world can never wrong her State.
> Lewis, thou shalt be bravely shipped to France,
> For never Frenchman got of English ground
> The twentieth part that thou hast conquered.
> Dauphin, thy hand: to Worcester we will march:
> Lords all, lay hands to bear your sovereign
> With obsequies of honour to his grave:
> If England's peers and people join in one,
> Nor Pope, nor France, nor Spain can do them wrong.

Shakespeare takes this weak patriotic speech out of its historical context by substituting "the three corners of the world in arms" for the Pope, France, and Spain. With a few adjustments, Shakespeare prefigures *Henry V* and concludes his play with one of his most stirring patriotic speeches:

> This England never did, nor never shall,
> Lie at the proud foot of a conqueror
> But when it first did help to wound itself.
> Now these her princes are come home again,
> Come the three corners of the world in arms,
> And we shall shock them! Naught shall make us rue
> If England to itself do rest but true!   (V.vii.112-118)

THE PROBLEMS OF HISTORY

King John tells the events of 1167-1216, with some Shakespearean alterations. King John became England's monarch on the death of his brother Richard I ("the Lionheart"), but he is mainly known today for being forced by the barons to accept Magna Charta (the basis of English freedom), signed at Runnymede. However, Shakespeare had more interest in the religious power struggle of John's reign.

The throne was claimed by Arthur (son of John's older brother, Geoffrey) with the military support of Philip II of France. In 1203 Arthur died in captivity, and rumour blamed John for his murder. In 1206 John defied Pope Innocent III's order to appoint Stephen Langton Archbishop of Canterbury. In 1208 the Pope excommunicated John, who, five years later, surrendered his crown to the papal legate. He then received it back again to symbolize that he held England in fief in the name of the Pope. After signing Magna Charta (1215), John fought again with the English barons, who were aided by France. John died in 1216 as the campaign continued, and he was succeeded by his nine-year-old son Henry III. In his play, Shakespeare used these historical events, making adjustments to the facts for a unified dramatic effect.

John has an ambiguous place in later history. Medieval chroniclers, all Catholic, saw him as a usurper, murderer, and heretic. In the sixteenth century, he was viewed as a Protestant martyr and a hero of English nationalism, as in John Bale's *Kynge Johan*. Shakespeare, typically, takes the middle road, so his characters become richer and deeper while he explores the intricate world of politics with extraordinary subtlety. But he does not continue the anti-papal views of Bale and Foxe. On balance, he tends to the Catholic view, and his portrayal of John is unsympathetic.

Behind *King John* lies the long shadow of Richard Coeur de Lion. Shakespeare heightens this figure into the myth of a good and heroic king who was honourable, wise, sympathetic, and spread his goodness over the land, like ancient vegetation gods. In history, John was the legitimate heir named by his dying brother, Richard I. John's claim to the throne was better than that of his nephew Arthur, because primogeniture was only one legal route to the crown. Shakespeare's play ignores these facts. In Act I, Shakespeare makes John a usurper and invents the story that Richard divided the kingdom among three heirs: his nephew, the child Arthur; his brother John; and his son, the illegitimate Faulconbridge.

THE KEY POLITICAL ISSUES

Shakespeare's invention raises the key political and moral question of the play: *what is the essential requirement for a king — the right (Arthur), possession (John), or character (Faulconbridge)?* By adding Faulconbridge's claim to the two genuine claims in history, Shakespeare increases the significance of the question. Faulconbridge is Richard's illegitimate son, who does not possess the crown and has no right to it. Yet he is "the very spirit of Plantagenet" (I.i.167), inheriting from his father the personal qualities of a better king than either John or Arthur. Thus Shakespeare can explore more deeply the moral, personal, and political issues of the play. He also expands his initial question to tackle two political problems that face people when, first, they are the subjects of a weak and inadequate king, and second, both Christian and Machiavellian principles are used in politics. These issues are focused in persons; that is, they arise from what people think and do during the course of the play.

All Shakespeare's early "weak-king" plays *(Henry VI, King John* and *Richard II)* have a similar kind of ambivalence. *Henry VI* is the least ambivalent. Our sympathies for people rapidly shift back and forth even within scenes. We are continually uncertain about whom to trust. When the audience experiences this shifting, it can be disconcerting. The Tudors believed strongly in the principles of hierarchical obedience and the Divine Right of Kings, but, with a weak king, these principles bring impossible dilemmas. People *in extremis* want to be honourable, but, as they cannot resolve the chaos this idealism would bring, they act pragmatically, continually asking questions but receiving no satisfactory answers. For the Elizabethans it was not permissible to have divided loyalties. But in *King John* loyalties are indeed divided. This problem also occupied the Puritans, for whom this split eventually resulted in a final division between king and conscience.

In *King John* the weak-king theme is overshadowed by a new political dilemma. By the 1590s in England, good Christians searched for ways they could come to terms with "policy." They sought an alternative political solution. *King John* shows the efforts made by good men and women to bridge the gap between the moral and the possible, between Christianity and Machiavellianism.

The attempt to bridge the gap is a radical change for Shakespeare. In the other early weak-king plays there is an endless emotional oscillation, a sense of futility, and no feeling of resolution. But in *King John* there is an alteration in the atmosphere. Now there is some hope. We feel there must be an answer to the dilemma, if only the people could find it. Shakespeare's solutions are his own, and he shifts the audience's sympathy for the king by intensifying the extremes. John becomes more heroic when he opposes the Cardinal, and even more villainous in his plans for Prince Arthur.

In this way, *King John* is a transitional play between Shakespeare's early English histories and the *Henry IV-V* cycle. The 1590s were a turning point in the public acceptance of a new view of political reality. *Henry VI* was written early in Shakespeare's career, when his attitude to politics primarily reflected Christianity and his youth. By the time he revises *King John* (c. 1594), Elizabethan political views are changing with the influence of Machiavelli, and so the play bridges the gap between the political attitudes of the pro-Christian *Henry VI* and the pro-Machiavellian *Henry IV-V* of the later 1590s. Indeed, not only is *King John* the odd play out of Shakespeare's sequence of English history, but it is a turning point in his thinking. He begins to appreciate the kind of creative Machiavellianism explored in *Henry IV* and then embodied in *Henry V*.

King John is a story of people caught in *realpolitik*. John's legal claim to the throne becomes irrelevant because Shakespeare structures the play around people more than political theory. The moral drama of *King John* is the conflict between selfish, ephemeral, fearful, greedy convention and hypocrisy on the one hand, and the clear-eyed, honest, humorous reality of Faulconbridge on the other. Shakespeare asks that the senseless *realpolitik* be judged dramatically; that is, not by theory or political adages but through dramatic action. To this end, he places the free spirit of "a good blunt fellow," Faulconbridge, next to all the moral and political corruption. Faulconbridge emerges as the most attractive character in the play, particularly as the strong spokesman for English nationalism.

STRUCTURE

King John tells its story quite plainly. Shakespeare even cuts out important historical events in order to make the narrative clear. But the structure of the play is highly complex. It is a fascinating experiment in which Shakespeare freely mixes historical data with pure fiction in an original way.

We should start by saying what *King John* is *not*. First, John is not the hero of the play. There is no real hero, although the nearest claimant is Faulconbridge. *The primary structure of the play consists of the story lines of each of the main characters.* In any history play, Shakespeare is mostly interested in the persons involved and how they explore events that test moral or political theory against psychological reality. In *King John*, Shakespeare is concerned in particular with John, Faulconbridge, Hubert, Arthur and the King of France. He threads the story of each one through the historical sequence; as he does so, he raises political issues.

Second, the political issues are *not* the primary structure. If they were, Shakespeare would have written a political treatise and not a play. In fact, *the political issues are a supporting structure to the audience's understanding of the people involved.* Shakespeare deals with political issues in terms of people: how we know is seen in the context of who we are. As the play begins, the political structure is unbalanced and demands resolution: which factor (right, possession, or character) is the essential ingredient for kingship?

Both the narrative and political structures are asymmetrical. At the start of the play, we may think that the crown should go to Arthur, to whom it belongs by birthright. But we have not met him. When we do, we doubt our first decision: we may be sympathetic to his youth and weakness, but his actions reverse our view because he agrees to "embrace ... love ... welcome" and "forgive" the Duke of Austria (II.i.11-12), who was the killer of King Richard, and is still wearing Richard's lion's cloak. Arthur is a pawn moved by an ambitious mother and ruthless, self-seeking foreigners. If he became king, it would be disastrous for England. Only later, in the scenes with Hubert, do we have empathy for him, and long before the end of the play, he is dead.

How does *King John* unify these two structures? It does so through a triple form that relies even less than usual on the Act and scene divisions of later editors:

- The First Movement gives a picture of the Tudor "Reformation hero" who, by opposing the Pope, was a symbol for Tudor nationalism; and Faulconbridge is a rough-and-ready young soldier who is determined to learn "policy" and how to use it (I.i.-III.ii).
- The Second Movement has a brilliant sketch of John's evil, unstable, cruel, and unscrupulous nature, based on both historical truth and the famous story of Hubert and Arthur (III.iii-IV.iii).
- The Third Movement tries to return the king to importance in the realm because, without Arthur, John is the undisputed rightful king, but he dies (V.i-V.vii).

The revolt of the barons is attributed not to John's tyranny but to the death of Arthur, of which he is guilty not in fact but in desire.

ACTION

The First Movement: The Strong John

The claims to the English throne are set out. John rejects the King of France's demand to relinquish his throne to Arthur. John judges the case of Richard I's illegitimate son, Philip Faulconbridge and his half-brother, Robert, forcing Philip to choose between his property and honour. He chooses the latter and John knights him (I.i).

Shakespeare starts by making King John a usurper. Chatillon, the French ambassador, calls him England's "borrowed majesty" (line 4) and states Arthur's case of primogeniture (Chatillon is a pleasing sketch for the French herald in *Henry V*). John replies angrily. He is no weakling here, because Chatillon must tell his king that England will fight.

> Be thou as lightning in the eyes of France;
> For ere thou canst report I will be there,
> The thunder of my cannon shall be heard.　　(24-26)

John boasts that by "our strong possession and our right" (line 39) he will keep the crown, but his mother, Queen Eleanor, confides the truth to him.

> Your strong possession much more than your right,
> Or else it must go wrong with you and me.
> So much my conscience whispers in your ear,
> Which none but heaven, and you and I, shall hear.
> 　　(40-43)

The Bastard, Philip Faulconbridge, and his half-brother Robert bring their dispute to King John. John is a fair judge, but the sub-text is ironic. John decides for the older brother in contrast to his own treatment of Arthur. Faulconbridge symbolizes the national situation. He has inherited an estate (the realm). Everyone knows the younger but legitimate Robert is the rightful heir, but, for lack of proof, he is being "legally" cheated (as Arthur is). Faulconbridge (unlike John) is not permitted to enjoy his dishonourably held estate. John makes him choose between "honour" ("reputation") and possessions. Typically, he chooses "honour," and his ambitious gamble immediately pays off. John knights him as "Sir Richard."

The young Faulconbridge is naive, uncalculating, decisive, and heedless of the consequences. He has little subtlety or insight: "I am I, howe'er I was begot" (line 175). He and John radically differ. Where John asks, "What follows if we disallow of this?" (line 16), Faulconbridge says at once, "I'll take my chance" (line 151). He gambles, exchanging false respectability for an honest reputation as a royal bastard — to which he has a right. He makes a proper choice for an improper reason

> though I will not practise to deceive,
> Yet, to avoid deceit I mean to learn.　　(214-215)

Hubert holds Angiers for the King of England, where John faces the forces of Arthur (the armies of France and Austria). In a compromise, they agree to a royal marriage of France and England. John will give up his lands in France, and Arthur will become an English noble (II.i.1-560).

Outside the walls of Angiers is the boy Arthur, with his mother Constance. Before King Philip of France and his son, Lewis the Dauphin, Arthur makes peace with the murderer of Richard I, the Duke of Austria, who supports Arthur's claim. John, Eleanor, Faulconbridge, and John's niece, Blanch of Spain, arrive. The two armies face one another. Philip charges that England by right belongs to Arthur (lines 89-109). John delivers strong threats. Both kings descend to verbal brawling. After an unresolved skirmish, all emerge from battle to have another war of words.

Hubert says Angiers will open its gates to the one who proves himself the rightful King of England. Hubert's is a commonsense position: "We are the King of England's subjects," and

> he that proves the King,
> To him will we prove loyal.   (267-271)

Hubert's arguments for neutrality are appealing, but his responses show he has no moral position at all. He does not act according to his best moral alternative but leaves the decision to brute force (the text does not say so, but this may be a plot between John and Hubert). The response of Faulconbridge to the situation is loyal and total, but he is inexperienced and not yet very perceptive. In his lack of selfishness he is morally superior to Hubert even if, like him, he leaves the decision to naked force. At least he will be involved on the side to which he is loyal.

Faulconbridge, who insults the Duke of Austria in asides, makes his first stab at politics with his "wild" proposal that the kings join forces against Angiers and then return to their quarrel. His comment "smacks it not something of the policy?" (line 396) shows his pride in his own political idea — a rash response of naive loyalty, but insane ruthlessness when John gives it royal sanction (does this play into the hands of John and Hubert?)

Hubert quickly makes an alternative proposal, that if Lewis and Blanch marry, thus making England and France allies, Angiers will open its gates to them all. John compromises, giving up his five French provinces in return for capturing Arthur (is this what John and Hubert have been plotting?) As in *The Troublesome Raigne,* John loses our good will by giving away the five provinces. But so does King Philip by deserting Arthur.

Faulconbridge acts like a commentator throughout, learning from these political stratagems. But he learns most of all from Blanch, who has a brief but vital role. Hubert's suggestion that she marry the Dauphin allows both kings to save face and give up their useless enmity. Lewis, a political opportunist, switches rapidly from enemy to lover — a contrast with the disgusted sincerity of Faulconbridge and the honesty of Blanch. She is a political pawn like Arthur, but she is as plain-spoken as Faulconbridge and without any loss of dignity or feminine propriety:

> Further I will not flatter you, my lord,
> That all I see in you is worthy love ...   (516-517)

When John asks for her formal assent, she says that she is

> bound in honour still to do
> What you in wisdom still vouchsafe to say.   (522-523)

For the first time "honour" means a lofty personal obligation. Blanch keeps this kind of honour, whatever the consequences are to her. Faulconbridge is silent, but, as his soliloquy shows, he learns. He also learns that the political affairs of the time are corrupt, mean and seedy.

> *Faulconbridge reviews events in his "Commodity" soliloquy*
> *— "Mad world! Mad kings! Mad composition!"*
> *(II.i.561-598).*

Once a naive young man, Faulconbridge is changed by experience. He finds that the right name for how Machiavels operate is "Commodity," meaning expediency and self-interest, that pervert "all indifferency ... direction, purpose, course, intent" (lines 579-580). Commodity turns the noblest ideas into ignoble acts. Once blindly loyal to the crown, he now sees a kind of madness in those about him. For the first time he grasps that John fights in a dishonourable cause:

> John, to stop Arthur's title in the whole,
> Hath willingly departed with a part.   (562-563)

Faulconbridge loathes his father's killer, Austria, but he is shocked at Philip who said "Let Right Be Done," then yielded to "that daily break-vow ... That smooth-fac'd gentleman, tickling Commodity":

> This bawd, this broker, this all-changing word,
> Clapped on the outward eye of fickle France,
> Hath drawn him from his own determined aid,
> From a resolved and honourable war,
> To a most base and vile-concluded peace.   (582-586)

His reaction to Philip is that of a disillusioned, sensitive youth:

> Not that I have the power to clutch my hand
> When his fair angels would salute my palm,
> But for my hand, as unattempted yet,
> Like a poor beggar raileth on the rich.
> Well, whiles I am a beggar, I will rail
> And say there is no sin but to be rich;
> And being rich, my virtue then shall be
> To say there is no vice but beggary.   (589-596)

Faulconbridge is learning. Even the way he uses the word "honour" has changed to the way used by Blanch. And he recognizes "Commodity" in himself:

> And why rail I on this commodity?
> But for because he hath not wooed me yet ... (587-588)

Here he is the theatrical ancestor of Prince Hal. Both understand honour in the same way, but they identify strongly with the "system." Faulconbridge, as John's trusted supporter, has compromised with "honour," so he thinks he is corrupt and condemns himself. For Elizabethans in the 1590s there had to be a place for conscience and truth in political life. But this belief was not absolute: truth changes in different contexts. Later in the play those who seem most guilty, like Hubert, prove to be humane. But the political "system," based on a corrupt king, remains corrupt whatever people do. Faulconbridge must learn that this corruption requires new political concepts. He begins from "gain" rather than "honour," and he has an unswerving if cynical acceptance of the Tudor belief in loyalty to the reigning monarch, corrupt or not —

> Since kings break faith upon commodity,
> Gain, be my lord — for I will worship thee!   (598-599)

He faces and accepts reality. Faulconbridge's remarkable soliloquy shows that human beings can live with a myth that is divorced from reality, a cynical compromise with Tudor doctrine; that illusion can be used to rise in the world. This principle affects all of Shakespeare's subsequent work, in which *fiction is a valid way to deal with existence* — a dramatic perspective that reconciles the realities of life with human aspiration.

> *John defies Pandulph's demand to appoint Stephen*
> *Langton as Archbishop of Canterbury. Pandulph excom-*
> *municates John and forces Philip to make war on him*
> *(III.i).*

> *John wins, captures Arthur, and Faulconbridge beheads*
> *Austria (III.ii).*

This sequence emphasizes the religious issue and its political and human consequences. At Angiers on the wedding day of Blanch and Lewis, Constance bewails the betrayal of Arthur. Constance was a favourite role in days gone by, but Mrs. Siddons herself tells us how difficult it is to play; "I believe it nearly impossible." This is due to the role's emotional intensity, the completeness with which the part must be imagined, and the unceasing concentration it demands. Several years later, it was these very qualities that were missing in Mrs. Sharpe's performance of the role, according to a grumbling Macready.*

Pandulph, representing the Pope, reveals the political rather than the religious interest of the Church in interfering in John's affairs. John's defiance of Pandulph has great dignity and power. Shakespeare radically alters John's speeches from *The Troublesome Raigne* so that John speaks to Pandulph with genuine force:

> What earthy name to interrogatories
> Can task the free breath of a sacred king?
> Thou canst not, Cardinal, devise a name
> So slight, unworthy, and ridiculous
> To charge me to an answer, as the Pope.
> Tell him this tale, and from the mouth of England
> Add thus much more: that no Italian priest
> Shall tithe or toll in our dominions;
> But as we, under God, are supreme head,
> So under Him, that great supremacy
> Where we do reign we will alone uphold,

---

* See Sprague (1964).

Without th' assistance of a mortal hand.
So tell the Pope, all reverence set apart
To him and his usurped authority.   (III.i.147-160)

John surprises us here. Earlier we had been ambivalent towards him. Now we are suddenly confronted with a new John, the anti-papal hero, the strong English king opposing Rome. Does John really change, or is this another stratagem? On the surface, John speaks with real conviction. Most likely the effect results from Shakespeare's editing of the earlier play. Whatever the case, our respect for John greatly increases.

Pandulph insists that Philip break his oath to John, and Philip undergoes a struggle of loyalties and his conscience. But his betrayal of Arthur is deeply ironic, and Philip's vows before God simply mask his anxiety at losing the wealth and power that the Lewis-Blanch marriage was to bring him.

The Second Movement: The Sinister John

John sends Faulconbridge to England to ransack the abbeys for funds, and persuades Hubert to kill Arthur (III.iii).

Pandulph foretells Arthur's death and tells Lewis, married to Blanch, that he can adopt Arthur's claim to the throne (III.iv).

The play's atmosphere becomes darker and more brooding. The break between the first two Movements occurs here, not at the change of locality [after Act III]. The tone of the play alters upon King John's victory. The mood is gloomy, and John is more sinister.

The change in Faulconbridge's manner, begun earlier, continues. He is now John's chief lieutenant. He is to follow John's orders and ransack the abbeys, and he responds with a new, if crude, commitment to "gain" —

Bell, book, and candle shall not drive me back
When gold and silver becks me to come on.

                              (III.iii.12-13)

John changes more radically. The anti-papal hero is now an insidious and revolting villain. At the moment of his victory, he plots Arthur's murder. Throughout this Movement John is an evil figure whom some consider worse even than Richard III, yet he does not have Richard's theatrical and artificial panache or his vicious sense of humour. Shakespeare makes his complicity in the death of Arthur more obvious than his sources do. But John's wickedness is done so badly and weakly that it is horrifying. As he appeals to Hubert to commit the crime, John is both creepy and cloying: intensely personal, very sensuous, and even affectionate. There is even a physical sensuality in the imagery he uses —

> Or if that thou couldst see me without eyes,
> Hear me without thine ears, and make reply
> Without a tongue, using conceit [thought] alone,
> Without eyes, ears, and harmful sound of words;
> Then, in despite of brooded watchful day,
> I would into thy bosom pour my thoughts.
> But, ah, I will not! Yet I love thee well,
> And, by my troth, I think thou lovest me well.
>
> (III.iii.48-55)

John is clumsy. He has done all the hinting necessary by this time, and he has no need to reveal his wishes any further to Hubert. But he does. After a number of false starts, he finally manages to speak plainly:

> KING: Good Hubert! Hubert, Hubert, throw thine eye
> On yon young boy. I'll tell thee what, my friend,
> He is a very serpent in my way,
> And wheresoe'er this foot of mine doth tread
> He lies before me. Dost thou understand me?
> Thou art his keeper.
> HUB: And I'll keep him so
> That he shall not offend your Majesty.
> KING: Death.
> HUB: My lord.
> KING: A grave.
> HUB: He shall not live.
> KING: Enough.
> I could be merry now. Hubert, I love thee.
> Well, I'll not say what I intend for thee.
>
> (III.iii.59-68)

We now know that Hubert is a monster: he will kill a small child to serve his master. John's evil is hideous because it is incompetent and so embarrassingly and clumsily human. John promises

Hubert a reward, but precisely what is unspecified. More ambiguous is the sinister irony of John's words to Arthur that Hubert will attend on him "with all true duty" (III.iii.73). Only John, Hubert, and the audience know what that duty is.

Hubert also learns during the play. In the kings' confrontation, Hubert tried to remain aloof from commitment. But now he is caught between allegiance to a tyrant and compassion for a child. John rightly says:

> O my gentle Hubert,
> We owe thee much! (III.iii.19-20)

John flatters Hubert, but in truth he likely owes him the capture of both Arthur and Angiers. John promises the reward due but wants one more service, Arthur's murder. Hubert cannot be neutral. He must be loyal.

> *At Northampton Castle, Arthur persuades Hubert not to blind him and to spare his life (IV.i).*

The Hubert-John and Hubert-Arthur scenes are united where Shakespeare works with the human and the physical rather than the abstract. But in these scenes no one is killed nor any blood shed; these come later.

The scene in which Hubert is to kill Arthur, but Arthur persuades Hubert not to blind or kill him, is rightly famous. The evocative symbols (intended murder, red-hot iron, and affectionate child) are very powerful. The scene catches us up in deep emotion. It is so heavy with pathos, indeed, that the director must take care the scene does not topple over into laughter. But played with theatrical sensitivity, it is very moving.

The scene differs in both tone and content from the parallel scene in *The Troublesome Raigne*, which is a medieval theological debate. In *King John*, Hubert's evil intentions crumble before Arthur's humanity. They speak the language not of theology but of feeling. When Hubert's "head did but ache," says Arthur,

> I knit my handkercher about your brows ....

> And with my hand at midnight held your head. (42-45)

Hubert's shift from murder to blinding is unexpected and may appear illogical. It is likely that Hubert plans an accidental death during torture. The stage action physically symbolizes the moral situation of the realm, since we hear of Hubert's "duty" as iron, and of human sympathy as the living eye that he must put out. The scene murmurs with menace as brute power (Hubert, hot irons, concealed accomplices) threatens power-less innocence (the child). With the red-hot iron near his eyes, Arthur says he "would drink my tears" and later, when Hubert tells him to hold his tongue,

> Hubert, the utterance of a brace of tongues
> Must needs want pleading for a pair of eyes.
> Let me not hold my tongue. Let me not, Hubert!
> Or, Hubert, if you will, cut out my tongue,
> So I may keep mine eyes.   (97-101)

The pain and pity in Hubert's response to the boy emphasizes his compassion. He has become like a father to him long before he relents.

With Arthur, Shakespeare has the same problem of creat-ing innocent virtue on the stage as he had with Blanch. Both are formal symbols of victimized goodness, with Arthur as inno-cence and Blanch as integrity. The playwright is less successful with Blanch, because he has less to work with. But Arthur is one of the most effective portrayals of childhood Shakespeare ever achieved. This scene, where Arthur's innocence and trust overwhelm Hubert's intention to murder him, is the emotional climax of the play. Perhaps the ultimate viciousness of "this iron age" (line 60) is when innocence (Arthur) recognizes that its own appearance must be suspected:

> Nay, you may think my love was crafty love,
> And call it cunning.   (53-54)

Hubert goes through his greatest change, from a cold mon-ster forced into an evil act, to a man of human compassion. Actors search vainly for prior evidence that this monster could have a change of heart. There is none. Virtually all the other major people operate through Commodity, but Hubert reaches the brink of an abyss, trembles there for a moment, and, under the child's influence, turns his back on evil and is saved. Hubert chooses humanity and mercy over "gain" and grows towards honesty and truth. His decision to spare Arthur is the choice of a higher duty over a lower, and he makes it *in extremis,* thereby providing a strong moral lesson for the present day. But Hubert is not yet ready to face complete moral truth. He is immediately involved in deceit, and he must lie to John because he is in "much danger" (line 133).

This whole scene results from John's evil, and he is about to face the worst moment of his reign when he yields to the Pope (in the next Movement). But Shakespeare, by making the Hubert-Arthur scene a second major depth for John, emphasizes his violent and unpredictable shifts. These lead the audience into extreme uncertainty.

After John's second coronation, the nobles ask for Arthur's release. He agrees. Hubert brings the (false) news of the boy's death. The nobles go to see. John, in fear, repents. Eleanor and Constance are dead. The Dauphin is to invade England. Faulconbridge arrives with Peter of Pomfret and then goes to pacify the nobles. John blames Hubert for urging Arthur's death but learns that he lives (IV.ii).

The evil of King John and its effects upon him are the focus of this scene. It begins with long speeches of protesting metaphors by the lords, all complaining at the folly of John's second coronation:

> To gild refinèd gold, to paint the lily,
> To throw a perfume on the violet,
> To smooth the ice, or add another hue
> Unto the rainbow, or with taper-light
> To seek the beauteous eye of Heaven to garnish,
> Is wasteful and ridiculous excess.   (11-16)

Shakespeare uses this sudden glut of rich imagery to show the lords' sarcasm. The metaphors refer to the second coronation, superfluous to them:

> In this the antique and well noted face
> Of plain old form is much disfigurèd;
> And, like a shifted wind unto a sail,
> It makes the course of thoughts to fetch about,
> Startles and frights consideration,
> Makes sound opinion sick and truth suspected,
> For putting on so new a fashioned robe.   (21-27)

"The old plain form" that is "much disfigurèd" is England under John. His response is extraordinary. He is absolutely silent, shivering in fright. When he tries to bribe the lords by granting any request, they ask him to free Arthur, whose imprisonment

Doth move the murmuring lips of discontent
To break into this dangerous argument.   (53-54)

John is not a genuine devil. Richard III remains Shakespeare's most complete villain: he grins with malicious glee, but John whines and cringes. He is the symbol of corruptible and corrupted humanity — far more repulsive because so near to our own inner selves. It seems virtually impossible that this sweating, panicking, and vile creature can be redeemed. As he is so utterly human, he can be, but we cannot yet anticipate how.

When Hubert brings the (false) news of Arthur's death (line 68), we in the audience find our feelings shifting again. We identify with the nobles in their fury as they march out. Yet we also stay in our seats to hear the unexpected news. We are on an emotional roller-coaster. The effect of the news on John is shattering. He is almost destroyed by fear which also leads him to repent Arthur's death. But no matter how hard he repents (and how hard is that?), he *is* guilty. His petrifying fear allows Shakespeare, here as nowhere else, to show us the diseased mind of a king plagued with uncertainties like ourselves. We witness an unpleasant picture as a grovelling, guilt-ridden John "repents" Arthur's murder after the stormy departure of the lords. It makes extraordinary demands upon the actor which only Sir Donald Wolfit on television, in my experience, has satisfied.

John is shocked with various sudden reports. France is invading, the English nobles are rebelling, and Queen Eleanor is dead. Her death is a great blow to John's mental stability. "What! Mother dead!" Peter gives a prophesy that John will yield the crown "ere the next Ascension-day at noon." John is terrified. He helplessly begs Faulconbridge to win back the lords, but he also reveals *who* and where he is: "My mother dead!" (line 181) he repeats. We begin to pity John, and are emotionally prepared for Hubert's revelation that Arthur is alive. This is our first positive feeling for John since he rebuffed the Cardinal. Now, John thinks, all is well: Arthur lives, the nobles will return, the French will stay at home, and everyone will once more be loyal and faithful subjects of a heroic Protestant king. All is suddenly reversed. It appears John is saved, but things are not quite like that.

> *As Arthur tries to escape, he leaps to his death.*
> *Faulconbridge finds the body. The lords blame Hubert and*
> *go to the Dauphin. Faulconbridge and Hubert meet*
> *(IV.iii).*

A minute later and all that John has gained is lost — yet the fault is still his. Arthur dies beneath the castle walls: "O me! my uncle's spirit is in these stones" (line 9). We are back on an emotional switchback. We identify with the fury of the lords at finding Arthur's body, but our feelings are so mixed that we really do not care if John is at fault.

The scene is superbly constructed. The body has not been found when the English lords reveal they have been in treasonable contact with Pandulph; their claim to outraged ideals was a lie. The body is found; the nobles justify themselves with superlatives of horror, but we wait for Faulconbridge's reaction. "Sir Richard, what think you?" Salisbury asks (line 41). His reply is,

> It is a damnèd and a bloody work,
> The graceless action of a heavy hand —
> If that it be the work of any hand.   (57-59)

His stress on the "If" does not satisfy the angry lords. Hubert arrives to say that Arthur lives. He believes this, but it is a lie to those who have just seen the body. As Hubert is defended from the nobles' violent anger by Faulconbridge, they stride off to join the Dauphin. Faulconbridge and Hubert face one another in a brief but telling scene. Faulconbridge is very suspicious of Hubert, who has the *appearance* of guilt, and he demands an answer: "Knew you of this fair work?" (line 116). He indicates his stand if the answer is yes:

> There is not yet so ugly a fiend of hell
> As thou shalt be, if thou didst kill this child.   (123-124)

He tells Hubert honestly, "I do suspect thee very grievously" (line 134). Faulconbridge has matured, and with real psychological insight, he needs only listen to the quality of Hubert's brief denial to accept it without question. Of the main characters, only the two who wish to abandon Commodity look at each other and realize what they have found.

The ambiguity of Faulconbridge's second soliloquy reflects the complexity of the issues, but he sees the need to act. He recognizes Arthur's right to the throne, and he knows the ques-

tion is now irrelevant. While "England" (the rightful king) is
dead, England (the country) suffers,

> and vast confusion waits,
> As doth a raven on a sick-fallen beast,
> The imminent decay of wrested pomp.   (152-154)

There is only one honourable choice for anyone who would
serve England: "I'll to the King" (line 157). In both soliloquies,
Faulconbridge is overwhelmed by the evil effects of "policy":
the first soliloquy was full of rage, then disillusionment; but this
soliloquy is a bitter lament on the corrupt moral condition of
political life:

> I am amazed, methinks, and lose my way
> Among the thorns and dangers of this world.
> How easy dost thou take all England up!
> From forth this morsel of dead royalty
> The life, the right and truth, of all this realm
> Is fled to heaven; and England now is left
> To tug and scamble and to part by th' teeth
> The unowed interest of proud-swelling state.
> Now for the bare-picked bone of majesty
> Doth doggèd war bristle his angry crest ...   (140-149)

While he uses Machiavellian tactics, Faulconbridge must avoid
bloodshed wherever possible. Yet he will strive to come out on
top by the most effective means.

The Third Movement: The Dying John

> *John yields the crown to Pandulph and receives it back
> under the Pope's authority. Pandulph will stop the French
> invasion. Faulconbridge tells John of Arthur's real death.
> John, ill, gives him the power to defend the realm (V.i).*

This Movement is more compact than the rest of the play,
because Shakespeare emphasizes John's desperate helplessness,
not his guilt, and Faulconbridge is more important than in *The
Troublesome Raigne*. Shakespeare makes John's submission to
Pandulph a *fait accompli* and thus more damning. In a brief but
effective scene, the relation of the king and Faulconbridge
changes after he delivers his bad news about Arthur:

> And wild amazement hurries up and down
> The little number of your doubtful friends.   (35-36)

Others are "doubtful friends," but he, a trustworthy and fearless friend, also suspects John's hand in the child's death,

> the jewel of life
> By some damned hand was robbed and ta'en away.
>
> (40-41)

"Some damned hand" is dangerously blunt. There is a rising climax when John once again tries to place the blame on Hubert. Tempers rise. Faulconbridge directly implies that John is responsible for the murder.

> KING: That villain Hubert told me he did live.
> FAUL: So, on my soul, he did, for aught he knew.
>
> (42-43)

Faulconbridge stops his attack momentarily. John cringes. England becomes uppermost in Faulconbridge's mind. He tries to rally John to ward off the invaders. John can no longer function as king, so he asks him to act "as if" he were a king to inspire the army. But John has abandoned his power to Rome and, glad just to have kept his throne, thinks he has secured a "happy peace" (line 63) with Lewis. Faulconbridge is horrified: "O inglorious league!" (line 65). He so overwhelms John that he gives his authority to Faulconbridge: "Have thou the ordering of this present time" (line 77).

This is a vital moment in the play. John is incapable of kingship. On his behalf Faulconbridge controls the realm. Will he usurp the crown and become a good king like his father? In his view, he must live in a corrupt world and try to replace the weak king tradition with the hero king, like his father. His stirring lines create the hero-king as though there is no question that this is what John *is* and *has been* from the start:

> Be great in act, as you have been in thought;
> Let not the world see fear and sad distrust
> Govern the motion of a kingly eye.
> Be stirring as the time; be fire with fire;
> Threaten the threatener, and outface the brow
> Of bragging horror. So shall inferior eyes,
> To borrow their behaviours from the great,
> Grow great by your example and put on
> The dauntless spirit of resolution.
> Away, and glister like the god of war
> When he intendeth to become the field.
> Show boldness and aspiring confidence! (45-56)

Here, in Shakespeare's first experiments with his ringing patriotic speech pattern, are the sounds of a past Richard and, perhaps, a future Faulconbridge.

> *At the French camp the Dauphin and Melun (a French lord) meet with the English nobles. Faulconbridge threatens Lewis with war on behalf of John, and Lewis accepts (V.ii).*

The English nobles pledge their "holy vow" to Lewis. Pandulph says that John is reconciled to Rome, and Lewis must return to France. He refuses. Faulconbridge arrives and speaks of the scope

> And warrant limited unto my tongue. (123)

His is a waiting game. When he knows the situation, he takes charge.

> Now hear our English King,
> For thus his royalty doth speak in me:
> He is prepared, and reason too he should.
> This apish and unmannerly approach,
> This harnessed masque and unadvisèd revel,
> This unhaired sauciness and boyish troops,
> The King doth smile at; and is well prepared
> To whip this dwarfish war, this pigmy arms,
> From out the circle of his territories. (128-136)

He speaks of "the gallant monarch" (line 148), "warlike John" (line 176), who "is prepared" (line 130), and who "doth smile" (line 134) at the invasion. Yet it is no false fiction. Faulconbridge speaks in the new royal manner.

> For your own ladies and pale-visaged maids,
> Like Amazons, come tripping after drums,
> Their thimbles into armèd gauntlets change,
> Their needles to lances, and their gentle hearts
> To fierce and bloody inclination. (154-158)

His patriotic speeches are Shakespeare's first use of iambic pentameters to create a new type of diction, an engaging kind of patriotic word-song. This music becomes a powerful instrument of political image-making in the English language. Beyond *Henry V*, this music erupts in the speeches of modern patriotic leaders as diverse as Lloyd George, Roosevelt, Kennedy and Churchill. With this diction, Faulconbridge turns

the cringing John into a hero-king who strikes fear into his enemies and swells the hearts of his subjects.

*John is so ill with fever that Faulconbridge orders him to
leave the field of battle (V.iii).*
This brief scene shows fiction against fact: against "warlike
John," the public image, we see the impotence of the man, not
the mask but the reality. His role is now completely transferred
to Faulconbridge.

*Melun, dying, tells the English lords the Dauphin has
betrayed them, and that they should beg John's forgiveness
(V.iv).*
As Salisbury says,
That misbegotten devil, Faulconbridge,
In spite of spite, alone upholds the day.   (4-5)
The dying Melun's confession is a shock: he breaks his oath
to the Dauphin, who broke an oath to the English nobles, who
broke an oath to John — the Dauphin intends to execute the
nobles when he wins the battle! Despite their "holy vow"
(IV.iii.67), they scuttle quickly back to John. How can true hon-
our be disentangled from such situation? Melun says he saves
the lives of the lords because of the love of "one Hubert"
(V.iv.40), and because he himself had an English grandfather.
Loyalty of such a personal, patriotic, and human kind stands
above the meaningless oaths of Commodity, "gain," or systems.
For Shakespeare, it is a return to sanity and true honour.
Melun's act stops the endless circle of dishonour, a gesture with
distinct overtones of Christian forgiveness.

*After a brief scene in the French camp, near Swinstead
Abbey (V.v) —*

Faulconbridge and Hubert meet (V.vi).
The two people who have lifted themselves above
Commodity come together in another splendid scene, when
Hubert tells Faulconbridge that John is dying. No time is wasted in describing John's health (he was poisoned by a monk
according to history as Shakespeare knew it) as Hubert subtly
tests the effect of the king's approaching death on

Faulconbridge. What Hubert wants to know is whether Faulconbridge will seize the throne. Hubert's "Who art thou?" (line 9) is the final question that must be settled. Faulconbridge's reply, "Who thou wilt," and the reminder of his Plantagenet blood, suggests to us that Shakespeare has been grooming Faulconbridge to become king. And, indeed, so he has. Arthur is dead, John is dying, and Faulconbridge is the obvious successor. It is all understated, but Hubert's implications are clear:

> I left him almost speechless, and broke out
> To acquaint you with this evil, that you might
> The better arm you to the sudden time.   (24-26)

Hubert wants him to have the throne, and so do we. Hubert foresees a struggle: "The lords are all come back" (line 33), but they must not gain control. Faulconbridge's response is a prayer, more for England than for himself:

> Withhold thine indignation, mighty heaven,
> And tempt us not to bear above our power!   (37-38)

His sights are set on the defence of the realm. He has in the floods lost "half my power this night" (line 39) and now faces the invaders with decimated forces. The invasion, not the succession, is his business at the moment. And the question is doubly untimely, for John is still "the King" (line 43).

> *John lies poisoned. The nobles return to court, bringing*
> *Prince Henry, John's son. Many of the English army have*
> *been drowned in a sudden flood, and Lewis is marching*
> *on the remainder. John dies. Salisbury says that Pandulph*
> *has arranged peace, and Lewis is leaving England.*
> *Faulconbridge kneels to the new King Henry (V.vii).*

King John is coming to his ignoble end, but he brings forth a kind of despairing poetry. Shakespeare tightens all the action around John's death. Although it does not have the magnificent poetry of Richard II's death, it becomes genuinely tragic through its language. John's last words, as he awaits Faulconbridge's news about the French forces, are:

> The tackle of my heart is cracked and burnt,
> And all the shrouds wherewith my life should sail
> Are turnèd to one thread, one little hair;
> My heart hath one poor string to stay it by,

> Which holds but till thy news be utterèd,
> And then all this thou seest is but a clod
> And module of confounded royalty.   (52-58)

As John finally dies miserably, listening to the news of England's losses, Faulconbridge pays him the compliment of telling him the bald truth:

> The Dauphin is preparing hitherward,
> Where God He knows how we shall answer him!
>
>   (59-60)

He then speaks the ultimate pledge of the squire to the dead hero:

> I do but stay behind
> To do the office for thee of revenge,
> And then my soul shall wait on thee to heaven.   (70-72)

With John dead, Faulconbridge starts to rally the defence, but it is not necessary, since Lewis has also suffered great losses and has sued for peace. All is ready for the final ending.

Shakespeare, however, surprises us. We think all that remains is for Faulconbridge to reach his decision. After all, he is the only kingly candidate left. But Shakespeare has not told us the historical fact that there is another heir. Prince Henry, King John's son [later Henry III], here makes his first appearance, almost by magic: "And brought Prince Henry in their company" (V.vi.34). This is the first mention of him. An Elizabethan audience might have expected it, but whether or not they did is not the point: in the play *as a play* it is a surprise ending. Even when Prince Henry is introduced, we know little about him. He sounds pleasant enough, but he could equally well be played as a weakling reminiscent of Arthur. How the role is played on stage will naturally affect Faulconbridge's decision. But we suspect that Shakespeare's aim is that he has just something of a royal character about him, for this will bring a triumphant ending. But this ambiguity in the Prince's role shows that we no longer concentrate only on the question of what qualifies a king, or even who should be the king, but on what Faulconbridge will do now.

In a world of Commodity, Faulconbridge's conception of honour has grown until he is capable of a self-denying loyalty to England; the most worthy of Richard's heirs repudiates personal ambition. It is inevitable, therefore, that he kneels to

Prince Henry at the end of the play. He renounces his recently established claim to the throne, preventing further civil war. True honour makes Faulconbridge the best of subjects in a unified England, and honour, in the logic of the play, is more important than the character of the king. Beneath all the rhetoric, an extraordinary thing has happened: Richard the Lionheart has been born again in his son, but he will not be king!

Faulconbridge's closing speech, with its ringing final couplet, is rightly famous. Sometimes dismissed as "Armada rhetoric," it can be moving if we face threats like the Armada. It was, for instance, heart-warming in G. Wilson Knight's performances in the black-out of London during World War II. The speech is only platitudinous if we take it out of its context. After all, the play has just shown the moral complexity of loyalty: that it is a self-denying acceptance of a higher duty. Faulconbridge is using his new patriotic diction applied to the whole play. The accession of Henry III, who promises well, allows *King John* to end on a heroic note. "The king is dead — long live the king!" In late Tudor terms the need for what Faulconbridge represents was very great, and few, if any, of Shakespeare's plays have a finer ending. It is one of the most rousing speeches in Shakespearean drama, one that can transform an audience into a cheering crowd —

> Come the three corners of the world in arms,
> And we shall shock them! Naught shall make us rue,
> If England to itself do rest but true!   (V.vii.116-118)

The sound rings in our ears as we leave the theatre.

This sound had a double irony in World War II. Churchill, who used this music in his speeches defying Hitler, had, like Faulconbridge centuries before him, been given absolute power to conduct the war. Once peace was assured, both abdicated this power for the sake of their country.

THE MAJOR ROLES

The main difficulty in reading *King John* is that the major roles — King John, Faulconbridge, and Hubert — all alter so radically in the play that we are not always certain what kind of person is speaking. The reader can rightly ask how a unified portrait can be found when the role changes so radically and so often. The answer is: by acting them.

King John specifically *needs to be read as a play.* Shakespeare created the roles for his friends in the Lord Chamberlain's Men to act. Actors *find* the "thread" of the person in performance, as Shakespeare intended. Readers must also put themselves in the character's shoes to discover the unity in a role.

KING JOHN

Not only is John the least kingly king that Shakespeare ever created, but he is an unpleasant creature whom it is difficult to like. Shakespeare has wisely given us the warm and adventurous Faulconbridge as a balance. Where Faulconbridge grows, John degenerates. Just as our emotions are intended to swing to and fro, so we identify with people alternately. John is weak, untruthful, unfaithful, timid, cowardly, miserable, dishonourable, ambitious, and loyal to no one but his mother. Faulconbridge is strong, truthful, faithful, adventurous, courageous, humorous, without personal ambition, honourable, and supremely loyal to his sovereign and to England. John's speech is circuitous and humdrum, but Faulconbridge is open, direct, and picturesque in speech, with a real flair for verbal expression. Neither is spiritual. John does not know what he believes in. Faulconbridge grows from egocentrism ("I am I") to a dedication to his king and country.

John vacillates between extremes. He begins as a usurper, but he is a strong, secure monarch, who is an unkingly king only to his enemies. He is a national hero when he flings the challenge back at Chatillon, and when he turns back Rome's threats. An Elizabethan audience would cheer. He was the only medieval King of England to defy the Pope. He calls the Cardinal a "meddling priest," saying that, if "all the kings of Christendom" desert him,

> Yet I alone, alone do me oppose
> Against the Pope.   (III.i.170-171)

From great heights, John plunges to enormous depths. He gives up the French provinces, plots to kill Arthur, and capitulates to Pandulph — as low as any English king could sink in the 1590s. Then, his mother dead, John has a mental collapse. His great weakness is his emotional dependence on his ambitious mother. He has never grown up. As he disintegrates, he hears about the invasion and he cries out:

> Where is my mother's care,
> That such an army could be drawn in France,
> And she not hear of it? (IV.ii.117-119)

When he repeats, "What! Mother dead!... My mother dead!" we begin to pity him. He regresses steadily until he cannot control either the realm or himself, and then succumbs to poison.

FAULCONBRIDGE

Faulconbridge is not tied to his mother. He obtains his father's name from her by his audacity. Her confession delights him.

> Madam, I would not wish a better father.
> Some sins do bear their privilege on earth,
> And so doth yours. (I.i.260-262)

He is one of Shakespeare's important experiments. Like the Vice, the young Faulconbridge is humorous, cynical, satirical; he points out the ironies in the actions of others. Faulconbridge is a soldier of fortune who sees life in a practical way: clear-eyed and intelligent, he is amused to look through others' "masks." His knighthood will not make him a fake nobleman —

> A foot of honour better than I was,
> But many a many foot of land the worse! (I.i.182-183)

He has a characteristic *élan:* he enjoys life's adventure and so accepts Queen Eleanor's offer:

> ELEAN: I like thee well. Wilt thou forsake thy fortune,
> Bequeath thy land to him, and follow me?
> I am a soldier and now bound to France.
> (I.i.148-150)

Of the major roles, actors have least problems with the changes of Faulconbridge: he is growing up, but in spurts. At first, he does not question larger issues or, indeed, himself, and "honour" is "reputation." His actions more than his words show that he places honour above material things. He chooses to give up his estate rather than to deny Richard as his father. He avoids deceit —

> For he is but a bastard to the time
> That doth not smack of observation.
> And so am I — whether I smack or no. (I.i.207-209)

By observation and by weighing all possibilities, he tries to work with the political system, to create the *semblance of order*, even if the political world focuses on Commodity. He gibes at the apoplectic Austria, but for some time we hear nothing from Faulconbridge. He listens. When Hubert proposes a marriage between Blanch and Lewis, and threatens a fight to the death if the match is declined, Faulconbridge explodes:

> Here's a stay
> That shakes the rotten carcass of old death
> Out of his rags! Here's a large mouth, indeed,
> That spits forth death and mountains, rocks and seas,
> Talks as familiarly of roaring lions
> As maids of thirteen do of puppy-dogs.
> What cannoneer begot this lusty blood?
> He speaks plain cannon — fire and smoke and bounce;
> He gives the bastinado [blow] with his tongue.
> Our ears are cudgelled; not a word of his
> But buffets better than a fist of France.
> Zounds! I was never so bethumped with words
> Since I first called my brother's father dad!
>
> (II.i.455-467)

From a blustering soldier he becomes a moral commentator with great self-awareness. His Commodity (expediency) soliloquy tests two opposing principles, scheming self-interest vs. loyalty to England (commodity vs. honour), and, by the end of the play, he synthesizes them. His growing patriotism arises from his sensitivity to the requirements of practical politics. He is John's most zealous partisan, but he finds the killing of Arthur "a damnèd and a bloody work" (IV.iii.57).

It becomes clear that he would make a perfect king, as when he substitutes for John. Yet his usurpation never becomes a concrete issue. He believes in that which exists, the concrete reality, and defends the integrity of the present order against all theory. He suspects an idea decked in "so new a fashion'd robe," and to him the whole is more important than any of its parts. Moral order can be maintained only through obedience to its symbol, the king, and so he brings Commodity into the service of honour. He gives his allegiance to John because John is, at this moment in time, the most efficient instrument for England's preservation. Shakespeare has from the start prepared us for his last change by packing his speech with energetic pictures of Elizabethan life — eel skins, puppy dogs, toasting irons, the traveler with "his toothpick at my worship's mess" (I.i.190), and many more. He develops a particular style of patriotic speech with a unique ring to it. He pledges his allegiance to the new king, Henry III, so that, by the end, Faulconbridge has been transformed from the Vice into an equally allegorical figure, the Patriot — transfigured almost into pure symbol.

HUBERT

Hubert, the "citizen" who speaks for Angiers, is the terrible Hubert de Burgh. He starts as a stock Elizabethan villain who seems uncommitted. But John wins *because* of Hubert's neutrality; anything else would have tipped the scales. As the kings are to destroy Angiers, Hubert has a new proposal which proves excellent for John. (Was it a plot? There's nothing in the script.) Then Hubert becomes John's tool to murder Arthur. He is the royal executioner, his the most deadly mask of evil. He is the most inhumane because he only obeys orders, as Nazis claimed they were mere cogs in a machine. But with Arthur, Hubert alters from an unthinking monster to a humanitarian. The scene is superbly written as Hubert is slowly "converted by the child." But his "monster" reputation goes before him. In anguish, John cries that Hubert's presence made him seek Arthur's death —

> How oft the sight of means to do ill deeds
> Make deeds ill done! Hadst not thou been by,
> A fellow by the hand of nature marked,
> Quoted, and signed to do a deed of shame,
> This murder had not come into my mind.
>
> (IV.ii.219-223)

Hubert is not to blame for the boy's death, but what John says might be true for him. The monster Hubert beside John might have triggered his act. The lords find Arthur's body and naturally assume that Hubert has fulfilled his expected role. But even monsters can change, and by the end of the play he is united with Faulconbridge in working for humanitarian ends.

ELEANOR AND CONSTANCE

Two jealous mothers are ambitious for their sons, Eleanor for King John, and Constance for the boy Arthur. Eleanor's cold ambition is not primarily maternal. She is selfish and worldly — and John is his mother's son. Constance is another kind of mother: utterly maternal, her focus is her hero-worship of her son, and her suffering. She is an ambitious, domineering harridan. No one can silence her, try as they may. John tries brutality ["Bedlam, have done" (II.i.183)], and even Arthur remonstrates with her ["Good my mother, peace!" (II.i.163)], but nothing keeps her quiet. She has an awesome power and is much given to curses. At Arthur's capture by John, her grief is nearly madness. Because she will not relent, they call her mad, but she is not. She "wishes to heaven" she were, in order to forget her grief. After Philip deserts her, she never ceases raging, and never comes to terms with political reality. When Philip says: "You are as fond of grief as of your child," she shows great tenderness.

> Grief fills the room up of my absent child:
> Lies in his bed, walks up and down with me,
> Puts on his pretty looks, repeats his words,
> Remembers me of all his gracious parts,
> Stuffs out his vacant garments with his form.
>
> (III.iv.93-97)

Then, tearing her hair, Constance makes her final exit. She is finally reported, appropriately, to have died "in a frenzy" (IV.ii.122).

PHILIP AND PANDULPH

Philip of France is a smiling hypocrite, a kind of minor Claudius. At first, Philip stands for Arthur's right. When he betrays Arthur, however, he becomes contemptible; he is governed by greed. Of all the corrupted he looks worst, because he wore a mask of honour. More than anyone else in the play, Philip opens Faulconbridge's eyes to political reality.

Cardinal Pandulph, it has been said, anticipates Polonius and Iago. He is the perfect example of insidious Commodity, because his profession consists of turning to his advantage each weakness and virtue of others. In his own words,

'Tis wonderful
What may be wrought out of their discontent.
(III.iv.178-179)

THE SIGNIFICANCE FOR SHAKESPEARE

King John is a restless play. It lies at the crossroads of many ideas, moods and styles in Shakespeare's development. We can see its significance for him by the way it plays in the theatre. Most memorable are the mad cursings of the bereaved Constance; the tension between Faulconbridge and both John and Hubert; and the pathos of the young Prince Arthur, whose volubility, charm, and sweet forgiveness lead Shakespeare almost into sentimentality. This human love and pathos are intensified by the hard world around the young prince. The contrast of the searches for power and love is the play's focus.

The verse is formal and regular, but the plot is not equally formalized, and its structure is unique. Shakespeare uses historical situations, altering them if necessary, to set up personal dilemmas. These dilemmas, like the Greek *agones,* are the core of the play, where people make life and death choices. Out of the choices the characters must make, the concept of a united England begins to shine.

Politically, too, the play is at a crossroads. Shakespeare in *Henry VI* wrestles with Christian values in the face of Machiavellian *realpolitik.* The latter wins in *Richard III*, and the result is horror and chaos. Sometime after he completes *King John,* Shakespeare creates his other English histories, in which an acceptable Machiavellianism finally emerges with Hal as Henry V. *King John* is transitional between the political issues of two large blocks of history plays. In *King John,* Shakespeare sets forth for the first time a way that the new political methods can work in the English context.

The political theme in *King John* is the interdependence of Tudor nationalism and internal unity, a matter of great concern at the time. Elizabethan topicality is the *métier* of Faulconbridge. It is in keeping with his adventurous spirit that Coeur de Lion's son should take over as spokesman for nationalism. The ordinary Elizabethan man (although Faulconbridge is no ordinary man) makes the monarch the rallying point for national unity. The people are the foundation of Elizabethan monarchy. Faulconbridge, with royal blood in his veins, speaks the words that should have been King John's.

In this play, too, Shakespeare realizes the enormity of being a king. The strain on Henry VI leads him to give up the crown, but on John it brings mental collapse and death. The new King Henry III acknowledges the awe-ful symbol of sovereignty as the foundation of all stability,

> What surety of the world, what hope, what stay,
>
> When this was now a king, and now is clay? (V.vii.68-69)

As a King, John is mortal and weak, but he is also the enduring image. Shakespeare, like Faulconbridge, gives his allegiance to the King, whoever he is. A king's human fallibilities are magnified by the awe, power, and curse of royalty. John has royalty but cannot live with it. Faulconbridge cannot have royalty but would do well with it. These ironies become reflected in the contrasts between Richard II and Bolingbroke, in the desire of Henry IV to visit Jerusalem, and in Hal's relations with his father. Faulconbridge learns in *King John*. So does Shakespeare.

TITUS ANDRONICUS

HORROR ON STAGE

Immensely popular in its time, *Titus Andronicus* is today seldom read or performed. It is a lurid horror play, crudely violent, a chamber of horrors that includes thirteen deaths, two mutilations, one violent rape, and a cannibal banquet at which Tamora, the Queen of the Goths, is fed a pie made out of the bodies of her two sons.

The play is so like modern horror comics that it is no wonder it is rarely staged. The most famous modern productions were at the Old Vic in 1923 and Stratford-upon-Avon in 1955. Both theatres staged the play only in order to complete the whole cycle of Shakespeare plays, and both went full-out to make the atrocities as blood curdling and spine-chilling as possible to ensure that at least a minimum number of audience members fainted.

The Peter Brook production (1955) had Laurence Olivier at his greatest in the title role. Bernard Levin said his performance was "not so much on the heroic scale as on a new scale entirely, the greatness of which has smashed all our measuring-rods and pressure-gauges to smithereens."* As the grizzled war-weary Roman general, Olivier was spellbinding, with enormous pathos and a sense of physicality unknown on the stage before. The gut-wrenching sounds as he hacked off his hand, and the remarkable body control of his spectacular death, took British audiences by storm. He was supported by Anthony Quayle as a revolting Aaron, but the Lavinia was disappointing. In his review for *The Observer,* Kenneth Tynan wrote: "Miss Vivien Leigh receives the news that she is about to be ravished on her hus-

---

* For theatre history, see Sprague (1944, 1953, 1964) and Sprague and Trewin (1970).

band's corpse with little more than the mild annoyance of one
who would have preferred foam rubber." Since that time, there
has been a claustrophobic television production (BBC TV 1988)
with Eileen Atkins relishing her role as a vicious Tamora.

The date of *Titus Andronicus* remains a mystery.
Shakespeare probably wrote it in the late 1580s and reworked
it, while revising *King John,* in 1593-1594. Perhaps *Titus* was his
first play. The First Quarto, lost until 1904 (when a copy was
found in the house of a Swedish post office clerk), was published in 1594 and reprinted in 1600 and 1611. The play was
included in the *First Folio* (1623), and it was listed by Francis
Meres (1598).

Shakespeare uses three main sources. First is the historian
Suetonius, or, perhaps, the sixteenth century historians who
took their material from him. Second, Shakespeare is indebted
to Ovid's tale of the rape of Philomel (*Metamorphoses*, Book 6)
as the basis for the rape of Lavinia, and there are passages in
the play that use Ovid's vivid metaphorical style. Third, the
structure of the play, the brutally sensational deeds, and the
atmosphere are taken from Seneca, whose Latin tragedies,
studied by Elizabethan schoolboys, were translated into English
by 1581. *Titus* uses Latin quotations from Seneca, and dark
deeds are done in walled-up, secret, and private places. We are
in an exclusively aristocratic but dank world where there is no
sky and little light. The climax, in which Titus executes his
fiendish revenge, may derive from Seneca's *Thyestes*. The slay-
ing of Alarbus (I.i.96-144), however, is possibly influenced by
the *Slaughter of the Innocents,* in the Coventry Mystery Cycle.

STRUCTURE AND PLOT

Before the Peter Brook production, some scholars made the
assumption that *Titus Andronicus* was not entirely by
Shakespeare. That is not so today. Although the play has an
uncharacteristically very straightforward structure, what
Shakespeare did with it is far from simple. Literary scholars
have said that the play is in two parts, a horror play and a
revenge play, or the fall of Titus and his revenge. But performance shows that this is not quite accurate.

Titus focuses on a crisis facing Rome. In practical theatre terms, *Titus Andronicus* divides naturally into three linear Movements. Like so many of Shakespeare's plays, its natural rhythm has little relation to the Acts and scenes given by later editors. In the theatre the play is revealed as moving between two dominant rhythms: from order to chaos and back to order. That these changes happen *within* scenes — in I.i and V.ii — is a sign of Shakespeare's immaturity.

* In the brief First Movement (I.i-I.i.233), there is one predominant rhythm: Rome is stable, and Titus is successful.

* The Second Movement is most of the play. After Titus refuses to become emperor and chooses the eldest son of the late emperor, Saturninus, over his brother, Bassianus, chaos appears. In a variety of rhythms, many hideous plots and acts occur as Titus' fortune is all downhill.

* At V.ii.147, Titus' revenge begins to work, and the Third Movement begins. The rhythm repeats that of the First Movement, order returning to Rome as Titus' son, Lucius, becomes emperor.

Fitting into this linear and rhythmical structure, there is a second spatial structure, an imaginative and poetic framework based on symbolic contrast. The major contrast is between Titus and the strength of the Roman family representing order based upon past traditions, as against the force of chaos centered on Tamora and her evil influence over others. Shakespeare sees order vs. chaos in terms of both the Elizabethan world order [see *End Notes*] and Ovid's symbols. In Ovid, when the state falls into disorder it changes itself and transforms its people to eagles, tigers, bulls, and bears. These images are echoed in Titus' metaphor, "Rome is but a wilderness of tigers" (III.i.54), and Lucius' description of Tamora as "that heinous tiger" (V.iii.195). Indeed, the play might be characterized as a study of the emergence of the beast in man. The savage rape and dismemberment of Lavinia, like the Ovidian rape of Lucrece (which Shakespeare refers to twice in the play), is a central symbol of moral and political disorder.

Unlike most Shakespearean plays, *Titus* has a unified *tone* throughout: an ominous Senecan gloom surrounds a plot that is a veritable extravaganza of blood and revenge. There are different story lines within its framework, but all are closely fitted to the order-chaos-order structure.

ACTION

The First Movement: Order

Victorious over the Goths, Titus Andronicus returns to Rome. His prisoners include their Queen Tamora; her sons, Alarbus, Demetrius, and Chiron; and her lover Aaron the Moor. Titus orders Alarbus killed as a sacrifice to the spirits of his dead sons. Saturninus and Bassianus, sons of the late emperor, are rivals for the succession (I.i.1-233).

There is a slow rhythm of inevitability throughout this Movement. The 1988 TV production used a slow drum-beat throughout. Rome is stable because it is supported by the patriotism, religious beliefs, and moral principles of the past. This order is exemplified by Roman family life and the victorious general Titus Andronicus.

The ritualistic opening scene introduces the theme of role-playing in the argument about whether Saturninus or Bassianus should take the role of emperor. The brothers agree that Titus shall choose between them.

Titus arrives in procession with his prisoners. In a remarkable reversal of stage tradition, this parade is not the usual jubilant affair. It is an impressive funeral procession for Titus' other sons who were killed in battle, with everyone dressed in black. Tamora's son, Alarbus, is sacrificed in the funeral ritual, which leads Tamora and her two remaining sons to plot their revenge against Titus. Titus' sons are buried in the family tomb.

The Second Movement: Chaos

Titus refuses to become emperor and chooses Saturninus, eldest son of the late emperor, over his brother, Bassianus. Saturninus becomes emperor (I.i.234-275).

Titus is welcomed to Rome by the tribunes, led by his brother Marcus Andronicus. They choose Titus as their new emperor. His superior qualifications are stressed by his brother's praise of him and by his own review of his accomplishments. Titus refuses the imperial throne because of his age.

Give me a staff of honour for mine age,
But not a sceptre to control the world:
Upright he held it, lords, that held it last.   (198-200)
His actions show him to be a man of honour and an ideal person for the role of emperor. He throws his support behind Saturninus, the elder but less worthy of the two, who says he wants to marry Titus' daughter, Lavinia, although he lusts after Tamora.

> *Saturninus denies Lavinia and makes Tamora his queen;*
> *violent chaos results. Lavinia is abducted by Bassianus.*
> *Titus pursues them, and he kills his own son Mutius for*
> *blocking his path. Saturninus resents Titus's influence*
> *and becomes a pawn in the evil designs of Tamora, her two*
> *sons, and Aaron (I.i.276-496).*

The plots to which Tamora and Aaron subject Titus are motivated by Tamora's desire for revenge on her enemy:

I'll find a day to massacre them all,
And raze their faction and their family,
The cruel father and his traitorous sons,
To whom I sued for my dear son's life.   (I.i.450-454)
But Shakespeare dramatizes this from Titus' point of view so that the audience understands it as a tragedy of suffering, a series of increasing *agones* in response to more and more vicious horrors.

Titus Andronicus is Shakespeare's earliest attempt at a tragic hero, based on the sequence of roles that Titus uses. This sequence establishes Titus' personality. This technique is only partially successful, and the actor of the role must be exceptionally skilled.

Aaron, on behalf of his mistress, Tamora, changes events into what she calls the "complot" of a "timeless tragedy" (II.iii.265). Titus becomes the suffering victim of Aaron's attack, which he makes theatrical by referring to the manifestations of his grief as "dumb shows," and by wishing to

Plot some device of further misery
To make us wondered at in time to come.
                                        (III.i.132, 135-136)

Titus suggests that his suffering should also be regarded as a role, one that can replace the first as a man of honour. But as his grief turns to frustration and despair, Titus moves into yet another role, the half-real, half crafty madness of Act IV. This role has highly mannered speech and behaviour, and begins to resemble the progress of the revenge tragedy hero:

> Acts of black night, abominable deeds,
> Complots of mischief, treason, villainies,
> Ruthful to hear, yet piteously performed ...   (V.i.64-66)

Shakespeare often uses the word "tragedy" in his early plays, mostly with its theatrical meaning, as a thing witnessed rather than read. Marcus says that "the gods delight in tragedies" (IV.i.60), echoing the ancient theme of man's life as a dramatic spectacle witnessed by the immortals.

> *Horror piles on horror. Chiron and Demetrius stab*
> *Bassianus, throw his body into a pit (a visual symbol of*
> *hell), rape Lavinia and, to keep her from identifying them,*
> *cut off her tongue and hands. Aaron tricks Martius and*
> *Quintus, sons of Titus, into the same pit; he convinces*
> *Saturninus they were the murderers of Bassianus, and*
> *they are condemned to death. Titus' third son, Lucius,*
> *tries to rescue them and is banished (II.i-III.i.59).*

Aaron the Moor, the most arresting figure in the play, exults in his passion for Tamora. He verbally achieves a grandeur reminiscent of Marlowe's heroic figures, notably Tamburlaine:

> Upon her wit doth earthly honour wait
> And virtue stoops and trembles at her frown.
> Then, Aaron, arm thy heart, and fit thy thoughts
> To mount aloft with thy imperial mistress ...
> Away with slavish weeds and servile thoughts!
> I will be bright, and shine in pearl and gold,
> To wait upon this new-made empress.
> To wait, said I? To wanton with this queen,
> This goddess, this Semiramis, this nymph ...   (II.i.10-22)

We remain distanced as one atrocity follows another. We may be aloof, surprised, or even amused, but we are never genuinely involved, for we are not helped by Shakespeare's artifi-

cial literary style. The ornamental imagery has no organic relationship to the events. When Martius falls into the pit and sees
Bassianus's corpse, he speaks incongruous embellishments:

> Upon his bloody finger he doth wear
> A precious ring that lightens all the hole,
> Which, like a taper in some monument,
> Doth shine upon the dead man's earthy cheeks,
> And shows the ragged entrails of the pit:
> So pale did shine the moon on Pyramus
> When he by night lay bathed in maiden blood.
> (II.iii.226-232)

But the most staggering incongruity is spoken by Marcus.
Shortly after the ghoulish stage direction, *Enter ... Lavinia, her
hands cut off, and her tongue cut out, and ravish'd,* Marcus says:

> Speak, gentle niece. What stern ungentle hand
> Hath lopp'd and hew'd and made thy body bare
> Of her two branches, those sweet ornaments
> Whose circling shadows kings have sought to sleep in,
> And might not gain so great a happiness
> As half thy love? Why dost not speak to me?
> Alas, a crimson river of warm blood,
> Like to a bubbling fountain stirr'd with wind,
> Doth rise and fall between thy rosed lips,
> Coming and going with thy honey breath.   (II.iv.16-25)

The contrast between the horror of the situation and the play-
fulness of the imagery is absurd and untragic. Marcus describes
Lavinia's bleeding mouth in a style close to Ovid's description
of the death of Pyramus, which Shakespeare used later in *The
Dream.* Yet this passage has no *dramatic* relevance: the action
stands still, and we cannot believe that Marcus is outraged and
torn by grief. In the 1988 TV production, however, Edward
Hardwicke managed to deliver these lines in all seriousness and
almost convinced the audience of his grief.

> *Aaron tells Titus the emperor will spare his sons if Titus,
> as a goodwill gesture, gives up his right hand. Titus does
> so, and Aaron sends the hand back with the severed heads
> of Martius and Quintus (III.i.60-240).*

> *Grotesquely, Lavinia turns the pages of Ovid with her*
> *stumps to find the story of Philomel. She places a staff in*
> *her mouth and between her stumps, to trace in the sand*
> *the names of her assailants (III.i.241-IV.i).*

Reading the words on the page cannot capture the gulf of horror into which we drop in the theatre. Lavinia's silent actions epitomize the play, and Titus' expression of grief is moving —

> For now I stand as one upon a rock,
> Environ'd with a wilderness of sea,
> Who marks the waxing tide grow wave by wave,
> Expecting ever when some envious surge
> Will in his brinish bowels swallow him.   (III.i.94-98)

From here, Titus plans his revenge, but unsuccessfully. His desperate appeals for justice prefigure Lear's, but he never matures into an acceptance of his sufferings. Rather, he becomes the Revenger.

> *Aaron and Tamora's black child is born; Aaron kills the*
> *nurse to keep the secret (IV.ii).*

Aaron the Moor "play'd the cheater" (V.i.111) for Titus' hand. A dissembler whose plots are theatrical, he shares Richard III's ghastly wit as he silences the nurse who was witness to the birth of his and Tamora's black child. Aaron says, "Weke, weke! So cries a pig prepared to the spit" (IV.ii.146), and stabs her. But he is not the actor that Richard of Gloucester is.

> *Titus shoots off arrows to the gods (IV.iii) as the Goths*
> *gather under Lucius (IV.iv.).*

> *The Goths capture Aaron who confesses his acts (V.i).*

When Aaron is asked, "Art thou not sorry for these heinous deeds?" he replies, "Ay, that I had not done a thousand more." He continues:

> Even now I curse the day (and yet I think
> Few come within the compass of my curse)
> Wherein I did not some notorious ill:
> As kill a man, or else devise his death;
> Ravish a maid, or plot the way to do it;
> Accuse some innocent, and forswear myself;

Set deadly enmity between two friends;
Make poor men's cattle break their necks;
Set fire on barns and hay-stacks in the night
And bid the owners quench them with their tears.
Oft have I digg'd up dead men from their graves
And set them upright at their dear friends' doors...
(V.i.125-136)

The result of this speech is a series of anticlimaxes, and in the end Aaron is ludicrous.

The Third Movement: Order

To begin his revenge, Titus slits the throats of Demetrius and Chiron as Lavinia holds a basin between her stumps to catch the blood (V.ii).

Titus, partly insane and partly feigning insanity, invites Tamora to a banquet and, dressed as a cook, places a dish before his guests. To end Lavinia's shame, he kills her and names Demetrius and Chiron as her defilers. He tells Tamora that she has been eating the flesh of her sons baked in a pie. Titus kills Tamora. Saturninus kills Titus. Lucius, back in Rome at the head of the Gothic army, kills Saturninus and becomes emperor (V.iii).

Titus takes command of the action and reverses its direction. From the tragedy of his suffering, initiated by Tamora and Aaron, he begins a genuine revenge tragedy. Yet he does not entirely control the action, which must follow its stereotypical course — to fulfil the revenge and be the death of the revenger.

Throughout, the action of the play is of plots and dumb shows and "timeless tragedies." These, with the visual presence of Tamora and her sons, disguised as Revenge attended by Rape and Murder, and also of Titus as a cook, give a highly theatrical, even melodramatic, effect. This theatrical imagery persuades the audience to see the play as a tragedy of suffering followed by a tragedy of revenge, with Titus passing through a series of roles. Revenger is his final role. There is also an attempt — first by Titus who compares himself to "rash Virginius" (V.iii.36), then by Marcus and Lucius in their eulogies of Titus — to re-establish Titus' first role, that of the man of perfect honour.

The play ends as it began, with preparations for the rites of burial. Order is restored to the city.

THE EFFECT OF VIOLENCE

Titus Andronicus, whatever its faults, shows a mastery of theatrical construction beyond the reach of any other contemporary Elizabethan dramatist, and some fine verse. But it is difficult to take the Grand Guignol seriously. It is not so much that the violence is excessive. After all, the atrocities in *King Lear* are almost as outrageous. *Titus* fails to reach tragic stature because it does not evoke real sympathy. Indeed, we can empathize with no one. In the theatre, we remain aloof as atrocities follow one another. We feel we are in the presence of series of tableaux, not of life itself.

These issues are comparable with what occurs with Thomas Kyd's *The Spanish Tragedy.* I have directed segments of *Titus* in rehearsal style, and I supervised Colin Skinner's experimental direction of Act IV of *The Spanish Tragedy* (University of Victoria, 1968), and they face a similar problem in the theatre: distancing the audience from the violence and brutality means that the director must take great care to prevent the horror from falling over into laughter.* In my view, a successful contemporary production of *Titus* requires a great actor, like Olivier, or heavy cuts to the text as took place at Stratford, Ontario, in 1989.

In reading the play, it is exciting to see the young Shakespeare flexing his dramatic muscles. In the theatre, what remains with us is not the language or the people: it is the visual image of the ravished Lavinia, her tongue cut out and white bandages covering her forearms, trying to write with a stick in the sand.

---

* Faber and Skinner (1970).

CONCLUSION

To direct Shakespeare's early history plays is not an easy task. It requires two fundamental skills. *First, an understanding of the historical and dramatic significance of the events in the play.* The director does not have to be an expert historian but must have a good grasp of the events that are to take place on the stage. This understanding includes the significance of the events within Shakespeare's dramaturgy; this may or may not coincide with their historical importance. Also required is an understanding of the social, economic and political events of Shakespeare's time; in many cases, the events in the plays reflect Elizabethan times as much as those of earlier history.

To direct Shakespeare's early history plays also requires, *second, an ability to use the Elizabethan unlocalized stage* [see *End Notes*]. The last thing the contemporary theatre requires is a front curtain going up and down while the scenery is changed, resulting in slow and ponderous productions. This may have been appropriate for Sir Henry Irving and other Victorian actors, but there have been great changes in the theatre during the last century. Nowhere has this change been more important than in the history plays.

On an unlocalized stage, armies can march in one door and out the other; or one army, down front, can watch other armies marching by through the doors at the rear of the stage. Thus Shakespeare's histories become a pageant of movement and colour, with processions, parades, solemn ceremonies, riots and battles all passing before us in splendour and vigorous action. The contrast with quiet, intimate scenes becomes a major stage effect; yet the actors in these scenes move onto the unlocalized stage with hardly any pause after a glorious parade has just exited. The whole production becomes, as Shakespeare envisaged it, one seamless web of dramatic action.

We have already seen the extraordinary genius of Shakespeare, the young dramatist, in creating these early histories at approximately the same period of his life as he created the early comedies. On the surface, there seems little to connect these two groups of plays except, of course, the masterly poetry that slowly emerges. But once you have worked with these plays in the theatre, another connection appears.

I have been fortunate enough to act in and direct various early histories and early comedies. Performing them on unlocalized stages gave me a practical insight into their unity. The dramatic movements, rhythms, pace and timing permitted by the unlocalized stage unify these early history plays with early comedies, discussed in *Shakespeare's Comic World*.

There is not so much large-group ceremonial in the comedies, but there are large-group festivities, such as the rambunctious wedding and the symmetrical finale in *The Taming of the Shrew*. Yet both the histories and the comedies are structured in duets, trios, quartets, or small groups. The modern director will discover similar structural patterns in the two kinds of play, patterns that are particularly effective on an unlocalized stage. The tone differs between history and comedy, but the way in which people come in and out, the swift pace (and alternative atmosphere) between scenes, the rhythms that roll on and on to catch up the audience in the excitement — these factors are an inherent part of both kinds of play. They set the standard for all that followed.

The Inigo Jones Theatre

Skin Market Tower

The Globe

Stage Machinery

Sculpture   Sculpture

Wishing Well

Sculptured Gates

Architect's drawing for the reconstruction of the Globe Theatre, Southwark, London, cut away to show the stage and heavens. The first plays will be staged during the Summer of 1995.

Project Architect:Theo Crosby, Pentagram Design, London.

END NOTES

ELIZABETHAN WORLD ORDER

Shakespeare's England is Christian. The English Reformation, begun by Henry VIII and continued by his daughter, Elizabeth I, establishes the Church of England (Anglican) as the official form of worship. But strong Catholic forces continue to work against the established church: the Armada, sent by Philip of Spain to restore Catholicism in England, is defeated in 1588, about the time Shakespeare arrives in London from Stratford-upon-Avon. Puritanism is also growing at this time.

Richard Hooker's great work defending the Anglican church, *Of the Laws of Ecclesiastical Polity,* says that God created the world according to a perfect plan. Each of his creations has a special function. As long as this order is preserved, the universe works beautifully and efficiently, with an orderly and permanent hierarchy, a chain of command from top to bottom. This chain is repeated in each realm of existence: thus God rules over the cosmos, the sun over the planets, the king over the body politic, the husband over the wife and family, the head over the other body parts, and so on. If this universal order is disturbed, chaos results — a great horror.

This view, derived from the male-oriented cultures of antiquity (Hittites, Israelites, Greeks, etc.), mixed with those aspects of Christianity encouraged by the Reformation.

The principle of order appears many times in Shakespeare's plays, most notably in Ulysses' speech on degree in *Troilus and Cressida* (I.iii.75-137), and Katherine's lecture to the other women on wifely submission at the end of *The Shrew* (V.ii.135-178) [see GENDER, below]. The breakdown of order is an offence against God: Macbeth's murder of Duncan, Paris's abduction of Helen from her lawful husband, the rejection of Lear by his daughters, Bolingbroke's overthrow of Richard II, and so on. The parallel of "king" to "sun" is used of Richard II, but not of Henry V because his father was a usurper, although Henry V is continually "golden."

PERSONALITY

A human being is a microcosm, a little world. His or her physical, mental and moral state resembles the macrocosm, somewhat like a hologram. The macrocosm can be seen as the body politic or as the universe. Both microcosm and macrocosm have four elements (fire, air, water, earth) which in people become four *humours:* blood, phlegm, yellow bile, and black bile. In Elizabethan psychology, they produce different "types" of people. These principles lie behind many comedies of the period (e.g., Ben Jonson's *Every Man in His Humour,* in which Shakespeare played a role), and they are inherent in many of Shakespeare's plays: e.g., Antony's final tribute to Brutus *(Julius Caesar,* V.v.68-75).

GENDER

Katherine's speech on wifely submission in *The Shrew* (V.ii.135-178) is a traditional Elizabethan view of the male-female relationship. This view is offensive to some modern feminists, but it must be understood in terms of Elizabethan mores. "Man" is the term used by Elizabethans for all human beings; females are clearly lesser beings. There is no reason to think that Shakespeare necessarily subscribed to this belief. It is true that throughout the plays he puts customary beliefs in the mouths of persons in the plays. Yet he often changes the traditional balance of males and females, particularly in the comedies, in which the woman may control the man (e.g., Helena, Rosalind) or be the focus of the action (Isabella, Portia). In this respect, Shakespeare is ahead of his contemporaries. Most of the tragedies, however, picture the female from the perspective of the male hero (e.g., Desdemona, Gertrude). The exception is *Antony and Cleopatra,* in which both have equal weight.

SOUL AND MIND

The Tudors use Aristotle's division of the soul into the vegetal, the sensible, and the rational faculties. The vegetal is shared by all living creatures and is responsible for the body's growth and generation. The sensible faculty, possessed by animals and people, is the source of feeling and motion. We perceive through the five senses. Perceptions are categorized by "the common sense," filtered through the imagination (fantasy), and ratified by reason.

Lack of imaginative control, as in illness, brings delusions. Delusions can also recur in sleep, when reason relaxes its vigilance, and Queen Mab gallops through the mind creating dreams *(Romeo & Juliet,* I.iv.53-103). Theseus in *The Dream* (V.i.4-22) shows that an unruly imagination is responsible for the erratic acts of lunatics, lovers, and poets. In this play the two pairs of lovers exemplify the delusions of unruly imagination.

TEXTS

The texts of Elizabethan dramatists were not exactly handled with care. The "Master of the Revels," a court official, examined each written script and often required moral or political revisions. The bookkeeper, or prompter, of the playhouse made the original manuscript (called "foul papers" or "fair copy") into a workable stage script (a "book") in which he wrote the cues, stage business, etc., together with any revisions or deletions made to satisfy the Master of the Revels. There were many such alterations, and sometimes the number of collaborators obscured the original author's intentions. Plays often remained in the repertory for a long time and could be revived periodically. Few plays were printed, because theatre managers were afraid that would reduce box-office receipts. Only forty or so of the two hundred or more plays performed between 1592 and 1603 have survived in print. Yet a reasonable reading public emerged for printed plays, usually in quarto editions.

Before 1623, nineteen of Shakespeare's plays had been published singly (in quarto), most more than once. Those printed from Shakespeare's own manuscripts, or from playhouse copies, are today called "good" quartos, while many "bad" quartos were pirated, often reconstructed from an actor's memory. *The First Folio,* in which Shakespeare's colleagues Hemmings and Condell collected most of his plays in one volume, was published in 1623 in a printing of about twelve hundred copies. It includes the engraving of Shakespeare by Martin Droeshout, a Flemish artist. This portrait is one of only two of Shakespeare known to be authentic; the other is the memorial bust in the Church of the Holy Trinity, Stratford.

SHAKESPEARE'S LANGUAGE

Elizabethan English is more flexible than the language of today. It has not settled down after its growth from Middle English into a modern form; it is not "fixed." For example, spelling is not uniform: the few existing examples of Shakespeare's signature show he even spells his name in different ways. He is not troubled by rigid rules of correctness, grammar, or definition. In addition to employing the common forms of his period, Shakespeare frequently uses language in his own distinctive way.

Elizabethan pronunciation is a matter of considerable scholarly debate. According to Kokeritz and others,* Shakespeare uses sounds similar to some modern English and American rural dialects: our *let* he pronounces *lit; virtue* as *vartue, nature* as *nater;* and *ea* like our *a* in t*a*le, so he said *speak* as *spake* and *dream* as *drame.* The noun *wind* could rhyme with either *kind* or *pinned.* Shakespeare sometimes makes two syllables of *-tion,* or adds a syllable to *Eng[e]land,* and at times makes a distinct syllable out of a final *-ed,* as in Antony's remark "The good is oft interrèd with their bones" (*Julius Caesar,* III.ii.77).

The verse basis of Shakespeare's plays is the iambic pentameter: iambic because there are two syllables with the accent on the second, and pentameter because there are five of them in a line, thus:
Te-TUM, te-TUM, te-TUM, te-TUM, te-TUM.
"And for I know she taketh most delight ... "
Shakespeare varies the beats in a line, and uses other line forms and prose, for dramatic effect. He uses rhyme more often in his early plays, to show artificiality, and can end a scene with a conventional rhyming couplet.

Renaissance writers have difficulty keeping pace with a language that is growing with the expansion of their social life. Shakespeare invents a vast range of words (e.g., assassination, disgraceful, gloomy, laughable, savagery) and combinations (e.g., falling to blows, an abrupt answer, bright and cheerful, sealing one's lips). More difficult for us are words that have changed their meaning or disappeared since Shakespeare used them. An example is "quibble," a game of "mis-taking the word": comic characters play it for fun, young lovers use it as a screen to hide their feelings

---

* See Kokeritz (1953) and Dobson (1968).

(like Beatrice and Benedick in *Much Ado)*, and it can communicate simultaneously on two or more levels, often with irony.

G. Wilson Knight emphasizes that each Shakespeare play is "a visionary unit bound to obey none but its own self-imposed laws ... as an expanded metaphor, by means of which the original vision has been projected into forms roughly correspondent with actuality."[*] Apart from the time-sequence which is the story, each play is unified in space (the play's "atmosphere") through imagery. Shakespeare's images cluster in groups; thus there are many nature images, particularly those relating to growing things in gardens and orchards, and there are repeated images in individual plays — light and dark in *Romeo and Juliet,* disease in *Hamlet,* animals in action in *Othello,* and so on. But imagery almost always refers to the whole play and cannot be separated from other elements.

THE PLAYHOUSE

Shakespeare writes for performances in the Theatre, the Globe, and other specific buildings. Information about the playhouses is disappointingly scarce, so modern reconstructions have been mostly conjecture; recent archeological discoveries in London have provided little more data. But we know enough about the *principles* of the Elizabethan and Jacobean theatre spaces to understand *why, what,* and *how* things took place.

THE "HOUSE" AND THE "PLACE"
The Elizabethan stage evolved from earlier forms. The liturgical drama and the massive medieval Cycles were based on two acting-areas: the "house," a localized space (a Paradise, a Hell, an ark for Noah, etc.); and the "place," a generalized space in front of one or more "houses."

The arrangement differed with the position of the "houses": in a line on a stage, as at Valençiennes; around a town square, as at Lucerne; on wagons wheeled from "place" to "place" ("stations"), as with some English Cycles; or in a circle with the audience in the middle, as in the Cornish and other English Cycles. In all cases, much of the action happened in the "place."

Interlude and Morality plays were normally performed by small professional troupes in the lord's hall. There the screen provided

---

[*] Knight (1957) 14-15.

an upper level, and on the ground level there were two doors on either side. On the wall between the doors was a "house" (sometimes a curtain) for entrances. The floor was the "place" where the actors performed. Single professional minstrels or small acting companies roamed far, performing in public streets, fields, taverns, and great houses. They set up the traditional booth stage of the old street theatre (a "house"), using any area around it as the "place."

In the sixteenth century, innyards were used. A wooden platform was built in the courtyard as a stage (the "place"), on which at least one "house" was probably sited. Spectators stood around, the stables became dressing rooms, and the several tiers of the gallery had seats for prosperous patrons. Some innkeepers in London and elsewhere found it profitable to lease their yards exclusively to theatrical companies. The playhouses used all these traditions, maintaining the localized "house" and the generalized "place."

THE PUBLIC PLAYHOUSES

In 1576 James Burbage built the Theatre, the first permanent playhouse in London, in the priory of Holywell, between Shoreditch High Street and Finsbury Fields. The site was just north of the city, outside the jurisdiction of the city authorities. In 1577 the Curtain was built nearby. In 1600 the manager, Philip Henslowe, with the actor Alleyn, built the Fortune, also to the north but west of Shoreditch. The Red Bull (c. 1605) was the last built to the north. An increasingly important area was Bankside, the south bank of the Thames, also beyond the control of the London council. On Bankside were built the Rose (c. 1587), the Swan (c. 1595), the Hope (1613), and in 1599 Burbage and his men transferred from the Theatre to the new Globe.

The professional companies were sponsored, but not financed, by prominent nobles. The Lord Chamberlain's Men owned and operated the Theatre and then the Globe; the company included Burbage, his son Richard, the famous actor, and Shakespeare. Their chief rival was the Lord Admiral's Men, managed by Henslowe. The principal actor of this company was Edward Alleyn, who created the role of Marlowe's Tamburlaine. The companies were continually harassed by the London burghers, who thought that the congregating mobs were a hazard to public health and law enforcement, and by Puritan agitators, like Stephen Gosson, who denounced theatres as inciting people to sin.

Popular stage from ancient times to Shakespeare's day: "house" and "place"

Two kinds of "house" and "place" in a medieval performance in the round

Interlude player in Tudor hall:
"house" is screen with two doors;
whole floor is "space"

Later adaptations to the medieval
hall: balcony at the top of the
screen; "tent" (curtains) set
against the centre of the screen

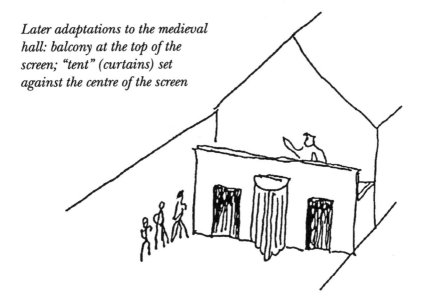

Conjectural Elizabethan playhouse (based on C. Walter Hodges); note the two doors and curtains for inner stage, plus upper stage, and trap door on the stage ("place")

The open air Elizabethan playhouse was usually round or polygonal, although the Fortune may have been rectangular. James Burbage, whose Theatre was probably a model for the rest, had previously built bear-pits and may have been influenced by his experience.

The stage area was built on the principle of the "house" and the "place." A bare platform jutted out into an unroofed yard or pit. At the rear of the platform was part of the main building, called the tiring house which had two purposes. Within it, the actors dressed. But the wall that separated the tiring house from the spectators was the façade that backed the stage. This façade had two doors on either side for entries and exits. Between them was either a recess with a draw curtain or a "house," and above was a gallery *(tarras)* where high scenes could be played. Although this was much like the staging for interludes, over the stage area was a roof (the "heavens") for possible descents, for making the noise of thunder, and for protecting the actors from the weather. Under the stage was the hell, or cellarage, from which devils and ghosts could rise through a trapdoor. "You hear this fellow in the cellarage," Hamlet says when the Ghost speaks from below (I.v.151).

Scenery as we know it hardly existed. There were large and small stage properties — a throne for a king, a bed for Desdemona, a tree for Malvolio — which were brought in and out in front of the audience, or "revealed" as the rear curtain was drawn. Atmospheric scene changes were done with words:

> But look, the morn, in russet mantle clad,
> Walks o'er the dew of yon high eastward hill.
>
> *(Hamlet,* I.i.167-168)

Costuming was splendid, but there was little attempt at historical accuracy. The simplicity of the stage allowed the dramatic action to move forward swiftly and continuously, and brought a physical closeness between actors and spectators, giving a special force to the aside and the soliloquy.

The groundlings stood in the pit. There were usually three tiers of gallery seats, which cost more. Gallants crowded onto the stage and might behave in a rowdy manner. The size of an Elizabethan audience averaged between two thousand and twenty five hundred. Johannes de Witt, a Dutch visitor who made the famous sketch of the Swan in 1596, said that it could seat three thousand, and there is no evidence to the contrary. Surrounded by gallants on the stage, groundlings in the pit, and the more affluent in the galleries, the actor appeared in the open air between the painted heavens above and the hell below.

THE "PRIVATE" THEATRES

Plays were also presented at the "private" theatres, often rented halls where more aristocratic artistic and moral traditions existed. Anyone could attend, but they catered to a small affluent group. These halls were roofed, well heated, and artificially lit, so they could be used in bad weather and at night.

Most housed troupes of children. Several London choir schools trained boys into expert actors in their own troupes; they were exploited on the commercial stage. These child troupes are not to be confused with the individual professional boy actors who took female roles in the adult troupes performing in the public playhouses.

When Hamlet asks why the players visiting Elsinore have left the city, Rosencrantz says they are victims of a "late innovation" (II.ii.332) of child troupes that has hurt their business:

> But there is, sir, an eyrie [nest] of children, little eyas-
> es [hawk chicks], that cry out on the top of question
> and are most tyrannically clapped for't. These are now
> the fashion, and so berattle the common stages (so
> they call them) that many wearing rapiers are afraid of
> goose-quills and dare scarce come thither.
>
> *(Hamlet,* II.ii.338-343)

That is, many Londoners did not attend the "private" theatres in case they were satirized by dramatists writing for the children's companies. Shakespeare's company gave winter performances in Blackfriars, a "private" theatre, after 1608.

THE DRAMATIC WORLD

"All the world's a stage," says Jaques. The comparison of the world with the stage, the *theatrum mundi,* runs throughout Shakespeare's works. He uses it in a variety of ways, changing its meaning from play to play. Although he did not invent the concept, he made it particularly his own.

DOUBLE MEANINGS

The "theatre of the world," the ancient play metaphor, is of great antiquity: it is used by Pythagoras, Plato, and Augustus Caesar; it occurs in Menander's *The Arbitrants,* and in Plautus and Terence, where characters, and by implication the audience, accept the *play world* as reality.*

In medieval England, the metaphor is used mostly in non-dramatic literature, as with Wyclif. Only in the sixteenth century, when the morality play becomes secular, do dramatists use the metaphor (based on Prudentius' *Psychomachia*) that acting is a disguise: the evil people in Skelton and Lyndsay change their names and clothes to seem honourable to their victims. Once actors are seen as dissemblers confusing honest men with illusion, comments about playing the "knave," or the "part," have a new and sinister quality. John Bale's play, *Kyng Johan* (c. 1539), is full of multiple changes of deceit.

The Vice survives on the Tudor secular stage. In early moralities he is a popular, accomplished rascal, a witty schemer, and a manipulator of the plot. He speaks to the onlookers using questions, insults, and mocking offers, which amuses them and keeps their attention. This brilliant figure joins "actor" to "deceiver," a double meaning taken up by the Puritans who see actors as hypocrites and counterfeits, people who persuade honest men of lies using names and costumes not their own. The Vice's audience address preserves the link between the players and the spectators. Play images cluster to him: in Heywood's *Play of Love* (c. 1532), the Vice pretends love for a woman he knows to be false; in *Ralph Roister Doister* (c. 1550), Merygreeke and Custance plan to gull the braggart by devising a playlet as a dramatist might plan a play; and Diccon, the Vice in *Gammer Gurton's Needle* (c. 1560), makes his mischievous plots dramatic.

Although the aside remains, the Vice's audience address and his clowning make his position in the play ambiguous, particularly when other people cannot overhear him. The final secularization of the theatre and the growth of the play as illusion allow the dramatic metaphor to enter English drama. In Gascoigne's play, *The Supposes* (1566), a character is astonished by a twist to the plot and suggests that "a man might make a Comedie of it" (V.vii.61-62). John Lyly's comedies, performed at court, no longer use the audience address, but prologues emphasize the dream-like nature of the play; the Prologue of *Sapho and Phao* (1584) asks the Queen to wake at the end of the performance. These traditions Shakespeare inherits.

---

* For references, see Righter (repr. 1967).

THE PLAY-WITHIN-THE-PLAY

The recognition of the theatrical nature of life originated in the medieval tradition and took form between 1550 and the work of Thomas Kyd, when the play establishes itself as illusion. Kyd's *The Spanish Tragedy* (c. 1589) deliberately builds on the metaphor of the world as a stage and creates "the play-within-the-play." Until then, experiments with this device were limited to *Fulgens and Lucres* and the anonymous *Rare Triumphs of Love and Fortune* (c. 1582). Kyd unites the medieval contact with the audience to the device of the self-sufficient play; but he does not use audience address. He relies on "the play-within-the-play" so extensively that the actual audience faces an image of itself: actors who sit as spectators within the play (actual vs. fictional; real Londoners vs. the imaginary court of Spain). This perspective becomes a major device of the time, and Shakespeare relies upon it.

When plays are first given in the new Theatre, the direct link of the audience and stage personages is renewed. Bridges between the real world (audience) and the *play world* are given by prologues, epilogues, and Chorus speeches, while within the play's action a bridge is provided by the aside and dramatic monologues. The audience address becomes the soliloquy; conventionally overheard by the spectators, it is not necessarily directed to them. For over half a century the soliloquy implies a deliberately vague relation of audience to personage, spectator to actor.

Many believe in the power that illusion has over reality. Hamlet says,

> The play's the thing
> Wherein I'll catch the conscience of the king.
>
> (II.ii.602-603)

This belief in the power of illusion is basic to the new relation between actors and audience, and to the effectiveness of the play metaphor. It could change people's lives. This belief continues with other dramatists: the citizen's wife of *The Knight of the Burning Pestle* (1607) and Jonson's poor gull in *Bartholomew Fair* (1614) are aware that the play they watch is only shadows, but then they forget. The play holds a mirror up to nature; it reflects the reality of its audience. But illusion affects the audience in many ways: some mistake illusion for reality, while others use the language and gestures of the theatre in the actual world.

THE METAPHOR IN SHAKESPEARE

Shakespeare combines direct and indirect references to the audience (e.g., *1 Henry IV*, V.iv.124-125; *Measure for Measure*, II.iv.9-10; *The Dream*, II.i.223-226) with the metaphor of the "theatre of the world." Shakespeare's play metaphors work in three related ways: they express the depth of the *play world;* they define the relation of that world to the actual world of the audience; and they show the illusion of ordinary life.

The association of the world with the stage builds itself deeply into his imagination and the structure of his plays. He uses play metaphors to a degree unusual even among his contemporaries.

Allied to the play metaphor is the use of boys for women's parts. In *Twelfth Night* and *As You Like It*, boys play the parts of girls who are acting the roles of boys. Rosalind is very conscious of this inversion, and Viola gently reminds us of gender differences.

A number of Shakespeare's characters function as dramatists within a play; they follow a dramatic plan towards a desired end. They differ in how they do so in two broad types, the actor-dramatist and the director-dramatist, those who act out their own dramatizations and those who manipulate others to perform events, as follows:

- *The actor-dramatist:* The actor-dramatist devises and acts out his own imagined dramas either because of self-delusion (Orsino) or in order to establish his bearings in a vast and chaotic universe (Lear).

  The actor-dramatist may include others in his own dramas, but he almost never forces them to play a part. Petruchio, for example, acts upon the rest of the characters as an actor-dramatist but acts as a director-dramatist when he manipulates Katherine. Othello is more extreme when he makes Desdemona fit into his drama by killing her.

- *The director-dramatist:* The director-dramatist knows what he is doing; he always has a firm goal. This kind of person plots with care before he acts, but, like Iago or Richard III, he often does so only one scene at a time. He functions with equal ease in comedy and tragedy and is related to the Vice, the clever slave servant of classical comedy, and the stage Machiavel. The most extreme kind, like Richard III, is a puppet master. The usual climax of his play is when he compels his victim to accept a new role. He is sometimes a subordinate character who initiates things or keeps them moving, bringing about the comic or tragic sufferings of the protagonists, as Pandarus and Sir Toby. But in *Richard III, Measure for Measure,* and *The Tempest,* he is the protagonist.

THE PLAYER KING

Queen Elizabeth I said that monarchs, like actors, stand on a stage in the sight of all the world, and the least blemish is visible to both enemies and friends. Shakespeare knew that the actual king sees in the player's performance an aspect of kingship itself. Then the juxtaposition of illusion and reality is enormously powerful and complex. The king at his coronation assumes a dramatic role, a part which he must interpret, but which he may not fundamentally change (Richard III cannot cope with this task). A king is identified with his dramatic role; he cannot be separated from it except by death or violence. He is the timeless and ideal symbol of things, the deputy of God on earth, the representative of the land and a people. He is a paradox: a particular person; and the embodiment of an abstract ideal. The pomp and ceremony that surround him are not an idle show; they distance him from the common reality, and they are the outward expression of authority. Form, tradition, ritual, dress, and procession make kingship visible.

The actor who plays the king is a greater paradox: he is a person and a player in the role of a king. In the trappings of royalty, he is a "mock king," like the ancient Whitsun monarch or Lord of Misrule. The Player King is a private man who sees his royalty as dream-like and insubstantial. When he takes off his crown and robes he is separated from his splendour and becomes "ordinary" again. In the history plays the Player King mechanically acts out the gestures of a role for which he is not suited (Henry VI, Richard III, Richard II, John), and he confronts an opposite who aspires to his role and who often helps his cause through the use of conscious role-playing (e.g., Richard Duke of York, Richard of Gloucester, Richmond, Bolingbroke, Faulconbridge).

THE PLAY AS DREAM

Shakespeare asks the audience to accept that the play is as important in their lives as their own dreams. He often uses "dream" and "play" synonymously; both are illusions. But as people in actual and fictional worlds have dreams, "dream" is a third reality distinct from those in which the audience and players live.

Dreams originate either inside or outside a person's consciousness, and can be of natural, diabolical, or divine origin. Sceptics think that dreams have natural, internal causes and do not foretell the future. A dream is caused by a disturbance in the imagination: the bodily spirits of the senses retain some images when they return to the heart, or brain, during sleep; they offer images to the imaginative faculty and produce dreams. According to George Chapman, imagination can be

stirr'd up by forms in the memory's store,
Or by the vapours of o'erflowing humours.
(*The Revenge of Bussy d'Ambois*, V.i.44-45)

Any disturbances in the normal balance of the bodily humours, the mind, indigestion, hunger, nervousness, or fear affect the imagination and are released in dream. Or, says Tourneur, dreams might be caused by

the raised
Impressions of premeditated things,
By serious apprehension left upon
Our minds.   (*The Atheist's Tragedy*, II.vi.29-32)

Hamlet calls dreams "a shadow" (II.ii.69), and Hastings, in *Richard III*, insists they are "the mockery of unquiet slumbers" (III.ii.27). Romeo says that dreamers "do dream things true" (I.iv.52), but Mercutio answers with his Queen Mab speech; dreams, he says, reveal the wishes of the dreamer. They

are the children of an idle brain,
Begot of nothing but vain fantasy.
(*Romeo & Juliet*, I.iv.97-98)

Imagination provides the dream with content, which consists of the events and worries of the actual world. It is memory more than fear or anguish that causes Lady Macbeth to sleepwalk. Richard III's dreams can be thought natural (they originate in Richard's memory), or divine (he is God's agent), or diabolical and supernatural (he is a devilish villain).

For Shakespeare, both malign and benign spirits exist. The malign are "objective evil": spirits, witches, ghosts, devils, demons, who project their power into nature and influence us but cannot change free will. They affect us from without, when they offer us a physical but insubstantial object (as evil spirits offer Macbeth a dagger); or from within, when they interfere with the humours to affect our senses. Dreams from spirits can lead us either to damnation or salvation. If benign, dreams warn us of future events. If malign, they delude us by playing on our desires — they deceive our imagination, fog our reason, and lead us to destruction. Shakespeare is ambivalent about the origin of dreams. He knows spirits exist, and that they affect the universe in storms (as in *The Tempest)*, in dreams (as in *Richard III)*, or are a mode of communication between the real and the spirit worlds (as in *Hamlet)*. People respond to dreams of their own free will. Hamlet and Macbeth are free to accept or reject the advice given in dream. Yet Shakespeare also knows that dreams of any origin are produced by the imagination, and no matter how real they seem, they are illusory.

Shakespeare consistently shows that, when people respond to dreams, their character is revealed by their choice. In the actual world, the *play world,* or the dream world, the individual's response to events tells us of his or her character. Lucullus, in *Timon of Athens,* and Shylock, in *The Merchant of Venice,* are the kind of people who would dream of riches, and they do, but their responses differ. Julius Caesar and Hector respond to their wives' dreams similarly. For Shakespeare, the dream is an imaginative reality. But who we are, and what we do in the actual world can affect our dreams: Hermia wakes up screaming in *The Dream* (II.ii.151-156); Katharine of Aragon, in *Henry VIII,* dreams a masque and responds in sleep with "signs of rejoicing"; and Richard III at Bosworth cries out in the actual world his dream-fears — "Give me another horse! Bind up my wounds! Have mercy, Jesu!" (V.iii.178-179) — that,

> Have struck more terror to the soul of Richard
> Than can the substance of ten thousand soldiers.

> (V.iii.218-219)

Dream may affect us in the actual world for any length of time: Christopher Sly, in *The Shrew,* thinks he has been in a dream for fifteen years; he sees his actual experience as dream. Richard II (V.i.18) and Katharine of Aragon *(Henry VIII,* II.iv.71) use dreams to cover a long period of happy time; and they wake to an unpleasant actuality. Similarly Henry V spurns Falstaff:

> I know thee not, old man. Fall to thy prayers.
> How ill white hairs become a fool and jester.
> I have long dreamt of such a kind of man,
> So surfeit-swelled, so old, and so profane,
> But being awaked I do despise my dream.

> *(2 Henry IV,* V.v.50-54)

His early adventures with Falstaff are now "my dream" (unreal and insubstantial), and he wakes to the actuality of kingship. This constant interchange of actual to dream, and vice versa, shows their vague boundaries.

Shakespeare thinks of the relation of the *play world* and the actual world much like the relation of the dream world and the *play world*. Hamlet equates the actor's art, and the world that art creates, with dream (II.ii.549); and Theseus says the play as a whole is a dream — "The best in this kind are but shadows; and the worst are no worse, if imagination amend them" *(The Dream,* V.i.208-209). Both figures in dreams and people in a play are shadows. Macbeth says,

> Life's but a walking shadow, a poor player
> That struts and frets his hour upon the stage,
> And then is heard no more.   (V.v.24-26)

The imagination bridges gaps between "worlds." The poet works imaginatively (as Theseus says) and has this faculty more than others. *Henry V* overcomes the gap between the actual world and the *play world* by prologues in which the Chorus constantly asks the audience to let the players "On your imaginary forces work" (I.Pro.18).

Shakespeare insists on the play's relevance to the lives of the spectators. He says it is a dream designed by the playwright, and the actor is the manipulator of that dream. It is then imaginatively re-created in the actual world by the audience.

The audience must understand that the play is not distinctly different from the actual world. A great play is not just to be enjoyed and forgotten but is a profound imaginative reality as relevant to their lives as their own dreams.

THE TUDOR MYTH

Elizabeth I was the granddaughter of Henry VII (Henry Tudor), the founder of the Tudor dynasty. As his claim to the throne was weak, two themes of the developing Tudor myth emphasized specific aspects of history. First, Henry VII claimed to be descended from King Arthur, fulfilling the prophecies of Cadwallader, last of the Briton kings — a story told by Leland and other chroniclers, and in Spenser's *Faerie Queene.* But second, Henry VII won the right to the crown at Bosworth, which also ended the tragic Lancaster-York feud in the Wars of the Roses.

This story was told by three main chroniclers: Polydore Vergil,

Edward Hall, and Raphael Holinshed, who saw the Wars as a pattern of cause-and-effect, murder-and-revenge, sin-and-punishment. England's guilt, which came about when Bolingbroke usurped the crown from the true king, Richard II, is transmitted down the generations (as in Aeschylean tragedy) until it is expiated at Bosworth where Richmond, before he kills Richard III, prays and sees himself as an agent of God's justice:

> O Thou, whose captain I account myself,
> Look on my forces with a gracious eye;
> Put in their hands Thy bruising irons of wrath,
> That they may crush down with a heavy fall
> Th' usurping helmets of our adversaries;
> Make us thy ministers of chastisement,
> That we may praise Thee in the victory.
>
> *(Richard III,* V.iii.109-115)

But Shakespeare tackles this civil strife in a peculiar order. He writes the plays about the last half first. It is only in the middle of the 1590s that he begins at the beginning. Richard II is the true but weak king who is overthrown by Bolingbroke of Lancaster in 1399; thus England is cursed by God to suffer until the rightful king is crowned. The reigns of Bolingbroke, as Henry IV, and his son, Henry V, follow.

Shakespeare began his early English histories with Henry V's death (1422). The young, weak son of Henry V, Henry VI, after years of factionalism and turbulence, is overthrown by the Yorkists: Edward II and then his brother, the villainous Richard III, killed at Bosworth by Henry Tudor in 1485.

For the Tudors, the break with the medieval line of succession when Richard II is deposed began an era of political disorder. Would a similar disorder happen on Elizabeth's death? Shakespeare focuses on the *role* of king — on the *symbol* of the crown — and he stresses its external theatricality. Henry VI uses it weakly, Richard III wickedly, so that the four early plays are one long tragedy: of England's collapse; of the people who fall; and of a role that no one can fill. The further away we are from Tudor times, the less the audience knows about the historical facts. But these are not of primary importance. Shakespeare sacrifices historical accuracy for dramatic effect to present us with enthralling people.

Each of the eight sequential plays of English history is a single unit. But created by one imagination, they make a coherent whole, often called epic in character — perhaps the only modern work that can be compared to Homer's epics. It has been said that its focus is not a single person but England: the decline and fall of the Plantagenets, with a prologue about King John and an epilogue on Henry VIII. The historical order of the reigns is less relevant to Shakespeare's imagination than the symbolic order. The plays begin with the greatest political confusion and national weakness under Richard II, and end after a great victory by a national hero (Henry VII).

There are differences in quality: only *Richard III* among the early histories compares with the glories of Shakespeare's second group. They have different structures; for each play he creates a new structure to fit a unique historical and political context. There is, for instance, a radical change with *Richard III:* a tighter structure is dominated by a magnetic person, and a whole new idea of the history play comes into being.

Nor does Shakespeare swallow the Tudor myth whole. He accepts the most important issue: Richmond's victory meant that God chose the Tudor monarchs to be his exalted deputies on earth, so obedience to the king is obedience to God. This Shakespeare re-creates as the principle of order in Ulysses' speech on degree *(Troilus and Cressida,* I.iii.75-137), and it is believed by Faulconbridge in *King John* and Richmond in *Richard III.*

But Shakespeare does not accept it completely. His histories have ambiguities, irony, and a dialogic process. His are not plays with "a message," that uncritically put forward specific moral ideas — Shakespeare in the histories is ambivalent about many ideas. His intuition goes beyond the morality of the Tudor myth to question it with sly, subtle ambiguities and even cast doubts on its human truth. He is writing not history but plays for the living stage. His success is evident when we see them today.

William Shakespeare was born in 1564 to a prosperous middle-class family in Stratford on Avon. By the age of thirty he was already well established in the London theatre scene. Around 1610 he retired to Stratford, where he died in 1616. The chronology below gives approximate dates the plays were written. From about 1588 to 1600 he wrote mainly history plays and comedies; from 1600 to 1608 tragedies and "dark" comedies, and from 1608 to 1612 dramatic romances.

Chronology of the Plays:

1588-1591	*2 Henry VI, 3 Henry VI*
1588-1594	*The Comedy of Errors, Love's Labour's Lost*
1590-1592	*1 Henry VI*
1590-1594	*Titus Andronicus, King John*
1592-1593	*Richard III*
1593-1594	*The Taming of the Shrew*
1593-1595	*The Two Gentlemen of Verona*
1594-1596	*Romeo and Juliet, A Midsummer Night's Dream*
1593-1595	*Richard II*
1594-1597	*The Merchant of Venice*
1597	*1 Henry IV*
1597-1598	*2 Henry IV*
1597-1601	*The Merry Wives of Windsor*
1598-1599	*Henry V*
1597-1600	*Much Ado About Nothing*
1599	*Julius Caesar*
1599-1600	*As You Like It, Twelfth Night*
1600-1601	*Hamlet*
1601-1602	*Troilus and Cressida*
1602-1604	*All's Well That Ends Well*
1602-1604	*Othello, Measure for Measure*
1604-1606	*King Lear, Macbeth*
1604-1608	*Timon of Athens*
1605-1607	*Antony and Cleopatra*
1606-1609	*Coriolanus*
1608-1609	*Pericles*
1609-1610	*Cymbeline*
1610-1611	*The Winter's Tale*
1611	*The Tempest*
1612-1613	*Henry VIII, Two Noble Kinsmen*

stratford 50
Festival of Canada
ARTISTIC DIRECTOR
RICHARD MONETTE

P.O. Box 520, Stratford, Ontario, Canada N5A 6V2
Courier only: 55 Queen Street, Stratford, Ontario N5A 4M9
E-mail: orders@stratfordfestival.ca • Long distance: (519) 273-1600 • Fax: (519) 273-6173

Bell FESTIVAL CONNECTION
VISITORS GUIDE · TICKETS · ACCOMMODATION
1·800·567·1600
www.stratfordfestival.ca

CONDITIONS OF SALE:
No refunds can be given for tickets returned. Tickets may be exchanged for another available performance, provided they are received by the Box Office at least 24 hours before the performance for which they were issued. A handling charge of $4 applies to each ticket exchanged. The management reserves the right to refund the purchase price and refuse admission. Programming, casting and schedule subject to change without notice. Exchanges are not permitted on day of performance.

IN THE INTERESTS OF ALL OUR PATRONS:
• Latecomers and people leaving the auditorium will not be seated until a suitable break in the performance, whereupon seating location will be at the discretion of the management. Because of the seating configurations at the Tom Patterson Theatre and Studio Theatre, it may not be possible to seat latecomers there until the interval.
• Cameras, tape recorders, personal stereos, pagers and cellular phones are not permitted inside the auditorium. Please check them at the House Manager's office in the lobby.
• No food or drink is permitted in the auditorium.
• Babes in arms will not be admitted to any performance.

ORCHESTRA
AISLE   LT
ROW   C
SEAT   4

1-SR
41-601427

RICHARD III : REIGN OF TERROR

** AVON THEATRE **
99 Downie Street, Stratford
WEDNESDAY SEPT 11/02 AT 2:00 PM
MATINEE

See reverse for conditions of sale
(Price) 32.38 + (Tax) 2.27 = 34.65
U Topping   AM   0037558

2002 stratford Festival of Canada 50
ARTISTIC DIRECTOR RICHARD MONETTE

ORCHESTRA
AISLE   LT
ROW   C
SEAT   4

RICHARD
SEP11M
34.65 SR1

stratford 50

Festival of Canada

ARTISTIC DIRECTOR
RICHARD MONETTE

Bell FESTIVAL CONNECTION

VISITORS' GUIDE • TICKETS • ACCOMMODATION

1·800·567·1600

www.stratfordfestival.ca

P.O. Box 520, Stratford, Ontario, Canada N5A 6V2

Courier only: 55 Queen Street, Stratford, Ontario N5A 4M9

E-mail: orders@stratfordfestival.ca • Long distance: (519) 273-1600 • Fax: (519) 273-6173

CONDITIONS OF SALE:

No refunds can be given for tickets returned. Tickets may be exchanged for another available performance, provided they are received by the Box Office at least 24 hours before the performance for which they were issued. A handling charge of $4 applies to each ticket exchanged. The management reserves the right to refund the purchase price and refuse admission. Programming, casting and schedule subject to change without notice. Exchanges are not permitted on day of performance.

IN THE INTERESTS OF ALL OUR PATRONS:

• Latecomers and people leaving the auditorium will not be seated until a suitable break in the performance, whereupon seating location will be at the discretion of the management. Because of the seating configurations at the Tom Patterson Theatre and Studio Theatre, it may not be possible to seat latecomers there until the interval.

• Cameras, tape recorders, personal stereos, pagers and cellular phones are not permitted inside the auditorium. Please check them at the House Manager's office in the lobby.

• No food or drink is permitted in the auditorium.

• Babes in arms will not be admitted to any performance.

ORCHESTRA
AISLE LT
ROW C
SEAT 5

1—5R
41—601427

RICHARD III : REIGN OF TERROR

** AVON THEATRE **
99 Downie Street, Stratford
WEDNESDAY SEPT 11/02 AT 2:00 PM
MATINEE

See reverse for conditions of sale
(Price) 32.38 + (Tax) 2.27 = 34.65
U Topping   Am   0037558

2002
stratford
Festival of Canada
ARTISTIC DIRECTOR RICHARD MONETTE
50

ORCHESTRA
AISLE LT
ROW C
SEAT 5

RICHARD
SEP11M
34.65 5R1

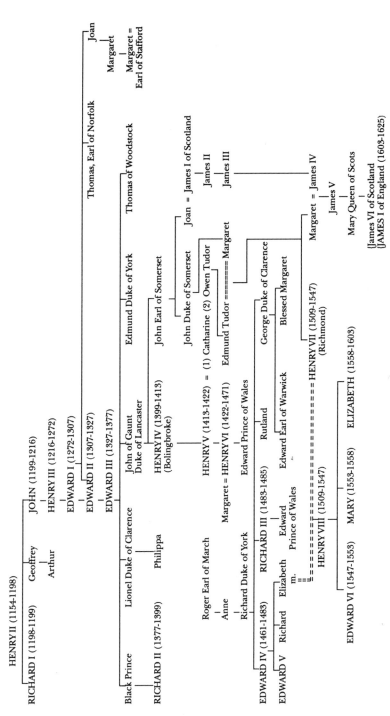

ENGLISH MONARCHS 1154-1625

WORKS RECOMMENDED
FOR STUDY
—— ALL VOLUMES ——

Beckerman, Bernard. *Shakespeare at the Globe 1599-1609*. London: Collier-Macmillan, 1962.

Bevington, David. *Action is Eloquence*. Cambridge: Harvard University Press, 1984.

Boas, F. S. *Shakespere and His Predecessors*. New York: Haskell House [1896], repr. 1968.

Bradbrook, Muriel C. *Shakespeare: The Poet in his World*. New York: Columbia University Press, 1978.

Bullough, Geoffrey. *Narrative and Dramatic Sources of Shakespeare*. 8 vols. New York: Columbia University Press, 1957-1975.

Calderwood, James L. *Shakespearean Metadrama*. Minneapolis: University of Minnesota Press, 1971.

Courtney, Richard. *Outline History of British Drama*. Totawa, N. J.: Littlefield, Adams, & Co., 1982.

Dollimore, Jonathan. *Radical Tragedy*. Chicago: University of Chicago Press, 1986.

Dollimore, Jonathan, and Alan Sinfield, eds. *Political Shakespeare*. Ithaca, N.Y.: Cornell University Press, 1985.

Ford, Boris, ed. *The Age of Shakespeare*. London: Cassell, 1961.

Frye, Northrop. *A Natural Perspective: The Development of Shakespearean Comedy and Romance*. New York: Columbia University Press, 1965.

—. *Fools of Time: Studies in Shakespearean Tragedy*. Toronto: University of Toronto Press, 1967.

—. *The Myth of Deliverance*. Toronto: University of Toronto Press, 1984.

—. *Northrop Frye on Shakespeare*. Toronto: Fitzhenry & Whiteside, 1986.

Gaster, T. H. *Thespis: Ritual, Myth and Drama in the Ancient Near-East*. New York: Doubleday, 2nd rev. ed., 1961.

Granville-Barker, Harley. *Prefaces to Shakespeare*. 4 vols. London: Batsford, repr. 1963.

Greenblatt, Stephen. *Renaissance Self-Fashioning*. Chicago: University of Chicago Press, 1980.

—. *Shakespearean Negotiations*. Berkeley and Los Angeles: University of California Press, 1988.

—. *Learning to Curse*. London: Routledge, 1990.

Howard, Jean E., and Marion F. O'Connor, eds. *Shakespeare Reproduced*. London: Methuen, 1987.

Kastan, David Scott, and Peter Stallybrass. *Staging the Renaissance*. London: Routledge, 1991.

Kinney, Arthur F., and Dan S. Collins, eds. *Renaissance Historicism*. Boston: University of Massachusetts, 1987.

Knight, G. Wilson. *Shakespearean Production*. London: Faber, 1964.

—. *Shakespeare and Religion*. London: Routledge and Kegan Paul, 1967.

Kott, Jan. *Shakespeare Our Contemporary*. Trans. B. Taborski. New York: Doubleday [1964], rev. 1967.

Leggatt, Alexander. *Shakespeare's Political Drama*. London: Routledge, 1988.

McGuire, Philip C., and David A. Samuelson. *Shakespeare: The Theatrical Dimension*. Washington: AMS Foundation, 1979.

Muir, Kenneth. *Shakespeare's Sources*. London: Methuen, 1957.

—. *Shakespeare the Professional*. Totawa, N. J.: Littlefield, Adams, & Co., 1973.

Nagler, A. M. *Shakespeare's Stage*. Trans. Ralph Manheim. New Haven: Yale University Press, 1958.

Oxford Companion to the Theatre and *Oxford Companion to the Canadian Theatre*. Toronto: Oxford University Press.

Righter, Anne. *Shakespeare and the Idea of the Play*. Harmondsworth: Penguin [1967], repr. 1982.

Salgado, Gamini. *Eyewitnesses to Shakespeare: First Hand Accounts of Performances 1590-1890*. London: Chatto & Windus, 1975.

Sinfield, Alan. *Faultlines*. Trans. Ralph Manheim. Berkeley and Los Angeles: University of California, 1992.

Slater, Ann Pasternak. *Shakespeare the Director*. New York: Barnes & Noble, 1982.

Sprague, Arthur Colby. *Shakespeare and the Actors*. Cambridge: Harvard University Press, 1944.

—. *Shakespearean Players and Performances*. Cambridge: Harvard University Press, 1953.

Sprague, Arthur Colby, and J. C. Trewin. *Shakespeare's Plays Today: Some Customs and Conventions of the Stage*. London: Sidgwick and Jackson, 1970.

Styan, J.L. *The Shakespeare Revolution*. Cambridge: Cambridge University Press, 1977.

Thomas, Brook. *New Historicism and Other Old-Fashioned Topics*. Princeton: Princeton University Press, 1991.

Van Laan, Thomas F. *Role-Playing in Shakespeare*. Toronto: University of Toronto Press, 1978.

Veeser, Aram, ed. *The New Historicism*. London: Routledge, 1989.

Wells, Stanley. *The Cambridge Companion to Shakespeare Studies*. Cambridge: Cambridge University Press, 1986.

Zesmer, David A. *Guide to Shakespeare*. New York: Barnes and Noble, 1976.

—— THE EARLY HISTORIES ——

Ashcroft, Peggy. Introduction, *Henry VI Parts 1, 2, 3.* London: The Folio Society, 1967.

Brown, John Russell, and Bernard Harris, eds. *Early Shakespeare.* London: Edward Arnold, 1961.

Dobson, E.J. *English Pronunciation, 1500-1700.* 2 vols. Oxford: The Clarendon Press, 2nd ed., 1968.

Eccles, Mark. "Richard III on Stage and Screen." In *Richard III,* 265-278. New York: Signet, 1965.

Eliot, T. S. "Shakespeare and the Stoicism of Seneca." In *Selected Essays 1917-1932.* New York: Harcourt, Brace, 1932.

Faber, M.D., and Colin Skinner. "The Spanish Tragedy: Act IV." *Philological Quarterly,* 49, 4 (October 1970): 444-459.

Hassel, R. Chris, Jr. *Songs of Death: Performance, Interpretation, and the Text of 'Richard III.'* Lincoln: University of Nebraska Press, 1987.

Jackson, Sir Barry. "On Producing 'Henry VI'." *Shakespeare Survey 6* (1953): 49-52.

Knight, G. Wilson. *The Wheel of Fire.* Cleveland and New York: World Publishing, Meridian, 5th rev. ed., 1957.

—. *The Sovereign Flower.* London: Methuen, 1958.

Kokeritz, Helge. *Shakespeare's Pronunciation.* New Haven: Yale University Press, 1953.

Manheim, Michael. *The Weak King Dilemma in Shakespearean History.* Syracuse, N. Y.: Syracuse University Press, 1973.

Nicoll, A. and J., eds. *Holinshed's Chronicle as Used in Shakespeare's Plays.* London: Dent, Everyman edition, 1927.

Prior, Moody E.. *The Drama of Power: Studies in Shakespeare's History Plays.* Evanston, Ill.: Northwestern University Press, 1973.

Richmond, Hugh M. *Shakespeare's Political Plays.* New York: Random House, 1967.

Righter, Anne. *Shakespeare and the Idea of the Play.* Harmondsworth: Penguin, repr. 1967.

Ryan, Lawrence V. "'Henry VI' on Stage and Screen." In *Henry VI Parts 1, 2, 3,* 230-250. New York: Signet, 1967

Sprague, Arthur Colby. *English Histories: Plays for the Stage.* London: Society for Theatre Research, 1964.

Tillyard, E. M. W. *Shakespeare's History Plays.* New York: Macmillan, 1946.

(Play texts quoted are from the Penguin Shakespeare series, published by Penguin Books Ltd., Harmondsworth, England.)

All's Well That Ends Well, copyright © 1970; Introduction, copyright © Barbara Everett, 1970.

As You Like It, copyright © 1968; Introduction, copyright © H.J. Oliver, 1968.

Antony and Cleopatra, copyright © 1977; Introduction, copyright © Emrys Jones, 1977.

The Comedy of Errors, copyright © 1972; Introduction, copyright © Stanley Wells, 1972.

Coriolanus, copyright © 1967; Introduction, copyright © G.R. Hibbard, 1967.

Cymbeline, not yet in print.

Hamlet, copyright © 1980; Introduction, copyright © Anne Barton, 1980.

1 Henry IV, copyright © 1968; Introduction, copyright © P.H. Davison, 1968.

2 Henry IV, copyright © 1977; Introduction, copyright © P.H. Davison, 1977.

Henry V, copyright © 1968; Introduction, copyright © A.R. Humphreys, 1968.

1 Henry VI, copyright © 1981; Introduction, copyright © Norman Sanders, 1981.

2 Henry VI, copyright © 1981; Introduction, copyright © Norman Sanders, 1981.

3 Henry VI, copyright © 1981; Introduction, copyright © Norman Sanders, 1981.

Henry VIII, copyright © 1971; Introduction, copyright © A.R. Humphreys, 1971.

Julius Caesar, copyright © 1967; Introduction, copyright © Norman Sanders, 1967.

King John, copyright © 1974; Introduction, copyright © R.L. Smallwood, 1974.

King Lear, copyright © 1972; Introduction, copyright © G.K. Hunter, 1972.

Love's Labour's Lost, copyright © 1982; Introduction, copyright © John Kerrigan, 1982.

Macbeth, copyright © 1977; Introduction, copyright © G.K. Hunter, 1977.

Measure for Measure, copyright © 1969; Introduction, copyright © J.M. Nosworthy, 1969.

The Merchant of Venice, copyright © 1967; Introduction, copyright © W. Moelwyn Merchant, 1967.

The Merry Wives of Windsor, copyright © 1973; Introduction, copyright © G.R. Hibbard, 1973.

Much Ado About Nothing, copyright © 1978; Introduction, copyright © R.A. Foakes, 1978.

A Midsummer Night's Dream, copyright © 1967; Introduction copyright © Stanley Wells, 1967.

Othello, copyright © 1968; Introduction, copyright © Kenneth Muir, 1968.